THE ABC OF MANAGEMENT

THE ABC OF MANAGEMENT
A Handbook of Management Terms and Concepts

John Blake and Peter Lawrence
Department of Management Studies
Loughborough University of Technology

CASSELL

Acknowledgements

We would like to thank several colleagues at the University of Loughborough for ideas and suggestions, including Bob Lee and Paul Finlay, and in particular Alan Bryman.

JB and PL

Cassell Educational Ltd
Artillery House
Artillery Row
London SW1P 1RT

First published 1989

British Library Cataloguing in Publication Data
Blake, John, *1950–*
The ABC of management.
1. Business firms. Management –
Encyclopaedias
I. Title   II. Lawrence, P.A. (Peter
Anthony, *1941–*
658′.003′21

ISBN 0 304 32228 8

Typeset by The Alden Press, London, Northampton and Oxford
Printed and bound in Great Britain by Biddles Ltd., Guilford

Preface

Everyone of us has some contact with management, whether as managers, as the managed, or most commonly as both. Management is not all a task performed successfully by those who bear the job title 'manager'. Many occupations involve substantial management responsibilities in situations where employers may have no awareness of a need for management training. For example, how many educational authorities provide any kind of management training opportunity for heads of departments in schools?

This book is aimed at managers at all levels. For the experienced and trained manager the book affords a useful refresher course, across the whole range of management disciplines, enriched by the authors' observations from their own research. For the manager without formal training who is determined to become professional, the book offers a comprehensive, readable and insightful introduction to the subject.

Alphabetical presentation has been chosen for two reasons. One is to make the book an easy-to-use work of reference. The other is to break down the traditional disciplinary sub-divisions of management education by presenting topics in what is effectively a random order. One entry, 1992, does not fit comfortably into such an order! This justified us in making 1992 the first entry. The challenge of 1992 is going to impose special demands on managers at all levels and in all sectors of the economy. We present the book in the hope that it will help to equip managers with the professionalism to meet the challenge.

Loughborough, June 1988

1992 The date that every manager in Europe should be aware of as both a golden opportunity and a major threat. Why? Because this is the date that the governments of the European Community have set as their deadline for the creation of a fully integrated European Internal Market. This means breaking down the notorious welter of 'non-tariff barriers' which obstruct the free movement of trade across national boundaries within the community. These restrictions include rules governing such areas as safety, health, the environment, production standards, and educational qualifications. The community will produce directives governing various types of product and service such that an enterprise complying with the appropriate directive will thereby gain access to all the markets of the community, i.e. some 320 million people, compared with some 236 million in the USA.

This has obvious implications for marketing strategy. Every company has an improved opportunity to market its product in other countries in the Community, and faces an increased challenge from competitors in those countries in the domestic market. There are equally important implications for other aspects of the manager's work. For example, workers will find it much easier to cross national boundaries in search of employment. In areas of skill shortage, managers will have the opportunity to recruit from other European countries, and face the prospect of seeing their own employees recruited by foreign competitors.

To face the challenge of 1992, managers will need to be aware of the implications of European Community harmonization for their own business. They will also need to equip themselves to meet the broader challenge of a more competitive environment. Specific points to consider in preparation for 1992 include:

- Which country offers the best location for the head office?

- Is it possible to improve the number of staff with language ability by a combination of training and recruitment policy?

- What changes need to be made in the marketing and sales network?

- Would the company be strengthened by a cross frontier merger within Europe?

- What opportunities are there for joint ventures with other European enterprises?

A

Absenteeism Absence from work for medical or other reasons. There is a basic distinction between involuntary absenteeism, usually the result of illness, and voluntary absenteeism deriving from disinclination to be at work. Having said this it is sometimes difficult to discriminate in practice, especially at the interface between minor illness and mild lead-swinging.

Absenteeism is an uneven phenomenon in the sense that rates often differ between industries and classes of worker. In Britain, for example, rates are higher among blue-collar workers than among white-collar workers; in jobs which are physically demanding and dangerous, such as coal-mining and deep-sea fishing, absenteeism may be a chosen way of reducing the strain, especially where workers feel they can stand the loss. There are also often pockets of absenteeism among working women who are also wives and mothers. In countries (the majority) in which no allowance is made for these commitments, looking after a sick husband or children may be tactically defined as the woman's own illness.

There are three senses in which absenteeism is important, especially for profit-making and manufacturing organizations. First, it disrupts the organization of production; this is acute in some industries, for example, in automobile companies where a production line cannot be started up at the beginning of a shift until it is manned. Second, absenteeism reduces capacity or predicted absenteeism forces up the level of manpower to have a built-in safety margin. Third, absenteeism depresses productivity, which is a ratio between employee input and saleable output.

It should be added that absenteeism is not only caused by illness and worker choice. There may also be structural causes, differing from country to country. Where military service, for instance, is a rolling incremental commitment as in Switzerland and Sweden, absenteeism rates are pushed up. Or again, to take a country with a high absenteeism rate, Sweden, where it is acknowledged to be around 20%, a major cause is the right of Swedish employees to take time out to attend full-time education courses.

Accountability A broad term implying both a responsibility for results and an obligation to report. Individual managers and the enterprise collectively may both be held 'accountable' to a range of parties. Accountability may be imposed internally, as when management holds a particular manager accountable for, say, plant safety. It may also be imposed externally, for example, when the law requires the directors to see that proper accounts are filed with the company registration officials. Managers should be aware of matters for which they personally are held accountable.

Accountant In both the USA and UK accountants occupy a central role in management. Most of them tend to be members of a professional body, and frequently have the most thorough training of the management team. At the same time, the accountant's training often involves an emphasis on how to comply with external requirements, e.g., company law and tax law. Thus there is a danger of the accountant identifying with the ethos of his profession rather than the ethos of the enterprise. We know at least one major multinational firm that trains its own accounting staff and actually discourages them from seeking membership of a professional accounting body.

The solution is for the accountant who takes on a management role to ensure that he acquires an equally professional grasp of management skills, possibly by some sort of formal training such as the MBA.

Accounting The most commonly quoted definition of accounting is that put forward by the American Accounting Association in 1966: 'The process of identifying, measuring, and communicating economic information to permit informed judgements and decisions by users of information'.

The definition is illuminating because it focuses on the decisions to be taken by the users of accounting information. This reveals one of the basic problems of accounting, that we have a variety of users each with different information needs. For example, the tax authorities will want to know the profit of a business, and they will want that profit to be computed on as objective a basis as possible. In contrast, the shareholders will want information that helps them assess the value of the company, and that may involve a range of subjective forecasts.

Thus the process of accounting measurement involves a compromise between different types of user need. Users of any accounting information should be aware of this, and interpret it accordingly. See also *cost accounting, financial accounting, management accounting.*

Acquisitions Acquisition of another business can have a number of benefits, including:

- This can be a fast way to acquire expertise in an area that the enterprise wants to enter.

- The combined enterprise may provide an improved share of the total market and so improve the competitive position.

- Cost savings may be achieved.

- Sometimes acquisitions can be picked up at a bargain price, for example, when the acquired company is on the verge of bankruptcy.

The major problem of acquisition is that it is often difficult to reconcile the different corporate culture of the acquired company with the rest of the enterprise. Acquisition can also give a spurious impression of growth, distracting management's attention from a low rate of internal development.

Action Learning An educational approach for managers developed in contrast to the traditional business school programmes. The most common type of action learning programme involves a group of four or five par-

3

ticipants each of whom faces a similar real-life problem in their own organization. The group is supported by a professional adviser who may be an educator or a consultant. The group meets periodically to work on the management problems they face, with the professional adviser acting not as a teacher but as a facilitator. Thus the members of the group learn primarily from each other's experience.

The basic principle of this approach is that managers have their best opportunities for development in their own organizations. A programme should develop managers' skills to recognize their existing experience for future problems. The approach has been advocated and developed with particular vigour by Professor Reg Revans.

Activity Trap   A situation that arises when managers or employees become so engrossed in the performance of assigned tasks that they lose sight of the reasons for performing the tasks. This leads to justification of activity by reference to the hard work put in rather than by results achieved. One way of avoiding the activity trap is to implement a system of *management by objectives* (see separate entry).

Ad hoc **Discussions**   The literature on management work stresses, quite rightly, the time managers spend at meetings, and makes the case for the development of 'meetings skills'. Below the level of more formal meetings, however, are briefer interactions which we term *ad hoc* discussions. These are not typically scheduled in advance as are more formal meetings, and involve smaller groups and simpler 'agendas' − one or two items rather than the standard formal beginning with minutes of the last meeting. *Ad hoc* discussions are a standard means for passing on up to the minute information; they are often triggered by a problem or crisis and so represent attempts to put right things that have gone wrong. *Ad hoc* discussions also 'cluster' a problem, that is, they may set in motion a series of such discussions over a short time period. *Ad hoc* discussions are sometimes precipitated by disagreements and personal antipathies, in the sense that where these cannot be contained in a formal meeting, someone may 'take out' the disagreements by means of *ad hoc* discussions with contenders separately, thereby manufacturing consensus off-stage. The frequency of *ad hoc* discussions is higher for junior rather than senior managers, and in smaller rather than larger companies. It is clear that some managers spend more time in this way than at formal meetings.

Administrative Man Theory   The starting point for understanding the theory of administrative man is in fact economic man. Economic man, as an abstraction to help us understand forces in economics, is held to consider all options rationally and to evaluate the consequences of all of them before making a decision. When he decides, he maximizes, taking the best of all options. As administrative science developed there was a tendency to take over the idea of economic man but this, in the view of American Nobel Prize winner Herbert Simon, is inappropriate. Administrative man cannnot behave in practice as economic man is supposed to in theory for two reasons:

(a) He suffers from cognitive limitations; administrative man is not a walking computer, he cannot keep all options and evaluated consequences in his mind, manipulating contrasted outcomes to facilitate a perfectly rational choice.

(b) Administrative man faces organizational and environmental constraints; he has to consider the political consequences of actions which may be inhibiting as well as the social limitations placed on his environment.

So what does administrative man do? He satisfices. He makes a reasonable, semi-rational choice in an imperfect (and imperfectly known) world. In short the notion of administrative man and his world of 'bounded rationality' serves to free us from the search for an unattainably perfect rationality of choice.

Advertising Advertising involves paying for messages about the product to be circulated in media owned and controlled by other people (see also *sales promotion*). Advertising is the aspect of marketing activity most immediately apparent to the general public, and it is important to remember:

- Advertising is only one part of the promotional mix (see *promotion*).

- In turn, promotion is only one part of the total marketing mix (see *marketing mix* and *four Ps*).

Advertising Standards Authority A body set up by all the major organizations concerned with advertising, representing advertisers, advertising agents and the media. It is financed by a levy on all advertising in the main media. The Advertising Standards Authority has issued a code of practice on advertising, the requirements being summarized as 'legal, decent, honest, and truthful'. The Authority exerts pressure for the amendment or withdrawal of advertisements contravening this code. Managers should be aware both of the need to comply with this code and the opportunity to complain of advertising activities by competitors which offend.

Advisory Conciliation and Arbitration Service Set up by the UK government in 1974, ACAS provides an independent *arbitration* and *mediation* (see separate entries) service for industrial disputes. ACAS has no legal powers of intervention, and can only be called in by the two parties to a dispute.

Advocacy Advocacy pervades a variety of management processes – making authority effective, making a success of lateral relations, handling subordinates, seeking to enhance power in the organization. The ability to plead, to make the case, is all important, whether it is done on paper, in open meetings, or face to face with individual seniors. Time and again the manager will want things – more resources, more co-operation, more time, more support – and these will only be obtainable through a cogent presentation of the case.

Affirmative Action   A term widely used in the USA for programmes to promote the hiring and advancement of groups that have traditionally suffered from discrimination in employment. US government support has included a requirement that firms undertaking government contract work should undertake such programmes. By contrast UK legislation tends to be confined to anti-discrimination measures.

Alienation   The concept was originated by Karl Marx, who held that under capitalism the worker is divorced from the fruits of his labour, in that:

- he does not own the means of production;

- he has to sell his labour;

- he is only producing a part of an end-product, not the whole; and hence experiences progressive alienation.

After Marx the term was used both more loosely and more pragmatically to signify dissatisfaction at work and loss of control. It has also been suggested that alienation is too global an idea, and that employee dissatisfaction has several independent components:

- powerlessness, or lack of control over the organization and conditions at work

- self-estrangement, in that the work is not a source of self-expression or self-fulfilment

- social isolation, in that the work does not lead to integrated work groups, membership of which is personally gratifying

- meaningless, in that tasks are frequently fragmented, short time-cycle contributions to a final product the individual worker never sees

The modern view tends to see technology rather than capitalism as the cause of alienation, noting that some technologies, for instance assembly-line production, are more alienating than others, such as process production technology with the greater control it affords the employee. To complete the picture there is a counter-argument which asserts that it is not so much the technology/kind of work which accounts for alienation as the expectations that employees bring to it. Thus the instrumental worker, as he has been identified in the research literature, who expects work to be unfulfilling and monotonous but provide the wherewithal for satisfaction outside work, may be 'happy in his way' and not in the classic sense alienated.

American Challenge, The   English title of *Le Défi Americain*, a major book urging a united European response to the challenge of US industrial domination. See under *Servan-Schreiber*, the author.

Appraisal The term refers to the formal appraisal of the performance of employees, usually at fixed time intervals. It is relatively rare for blue-collar workers to be appraised in this sense; here the emphasis is rather on job evaluation, to determine the distribution of pay awards by job demand or to allocate workers to work-pay categories. It is among white-collar workers, and especially in white-collar organizations such as banks and insurance companies, that appraisal schemes flourish, as well as of course among managers.

The appraisal is usually made by the subject's immediate boss, who typically makes assessments using variable grades such as 'unsatisfactory' to 'outstanding' on a 1 to 7 scale or whatever. These assessments again are usually made under prescribed headings such as 'punctuality', 'job knowledge' or 'initiative', and the appraisal form often concludes with a general assessment of the subject. It is normal for the subject to be informed of the assessment, indeed he or she often has to countersign it. The appraisal is frequently, in fact, a dialogue between the subject and the person making the assessment.

Employee appraisal has become more widespread in the 'value for money' climate of the 1980s. The case for appraisal includes:

- It represents feedback on performance of a formal kind, as opposed to the subject's impressions together with random bits of praise and blame over the year.

- Subjects frequently welcome the introduction of appraisal schemes, where the appraisal interview gives them a chance to say their piece and have the boss's real attention.

- The appraisal system may motivate employees.

- Employees may also be motivated to perform well because their promotion prospects are significantly dependent on the grades and quality of assessment achieved in appraisal.

- Again motivation may be enhanced where pay increments or a variable portion of the subject's remuneration is appraisal dependent.

- The institution of an appraisal system where the necessary spelling out of desired properties and dimensions of achievement may help the organization to focus on 'the kind of business it is in' and what is needed to do this well.

- Appraisal may make a contribution to career development by enabling the organization to play the strengths and compensate for the weaknesses of its members in the way it deploys them.

It is only fair to say that there are some potential dangers associated with appraisal.

- Bias or favouritism may occur on the part of the assessor.

- 'Grade drift' may occur, where 'very good' comes to mean average and 'satisfactory' means ought to have been fired last year.

- Goal displacement may occur, where subjects 'go for the grades' rather than go for excellent performance; there are sometimes opportunities to manipulate the system to get better grades.

- Appraisal systems tend to favour the well-rounded subject who gets a 'very good' on three dimensions and 'good' on the other four, though it may be the case that the performance of the person with one 'outstanding' and six 'satisfactories' is more valuable to the organization.

- Appraisal takes time, so that a price is being paid in terms of opportunity costs.

Arbitration   Agreements of various kinds often include a provision whereby in the event of a disagreement between the parties a neutral party will be called in to resolve the conflict. In ordinary commercial contracts arbitration can be used to cut costs of litigation. Arbitration is often used to resolve conflicts between management and unions. See also *pendulum arbitration*.

Argyris, Chris   American social scientist and protagonist of the self-actualizing view of man (see *Maslow's need hierarchy* and *neo-human relations*). Argyris' view is that man has a need for self-fulfilment, which is frustrated by the unrewarding nature of much work in modern industrial society (see *alienation*). So, Argyris is for:

- treating the worker as a human being, not so much in the sense of treating him decently but in recognizing the wholeness of his personality;

- allowing self-actualization at work;

- providing work which is meaningful to those engaged in it.

In more practical terms, the presumptive implications of Argyris' philosophy are job enlargement together with participation in the American sense of more involvement in workplace decision-making.

Aspirations   Worker representatives and trade union negotiators often refer to the aspirations of those they represent, especially in a bargaining situation. The expression has two overlapping meanings. First, it is sometimes a euphemism for what employees expect in terms of a pay rise and has the implication of 'we can't go back and offer the lads 3% if their aspirations are for 7%'. But increasingly the second meaning of the term has come to prevail, in the sense of non-monetary hopes, say for advancement, promotion, enhanced leisure enjoyment, or participation at work, which, it is implied, deserve to be recognized in the bargaining situation. Management needs to understand this, and can sometimes profit in negotiations by:

- Taking the initiative (not waiting for unreasonable demands)

- really doing something on the non-monetary side
- going for 'trade-offs'

Assertiveness Training A form of training designed to help people concerned in confrontations. Participants are trained to be assertive, by taking into account both their own and other people's feelings in a way that preserves the self-esteem of all concerned. The training method is normally by *role play* (see separate entry) of situations where assertion can be difficult. Managers concerned in handling staff in such situations as disciplinary interviews can find such training particularly useful. Those concerned in promoting equal opportunities, particularly for women in traditionally male-dominated roles, have also found that assertiveness training can help those confronted with prejudice.

Assessment Centre An approach to the identification of managerial potential which was developed in the late 1950s. The procedure of the assessment centre involves subjecting prospective managers to a wide variety of tests and interviews in order to assess skills and traits which are deemed to be predictive of managerial ability. The assessment centre is often used as a component in the development of existing managers as well. The standard ingredients of assessment centre testing, which is done intensively for a short period to highlight the managerial potential of subjects, are:

- in-basket or in-tray exercises
- business games
- group discussion
- projective tests (the essence of a projective test is that the subject has to reveal something of him or herself by responding to open ended stimuli of the 'failure is . . .' type)

The most famous and sustained use of assessment centre methods was that of the American Telephone and Telegraph Company. The Company had cohorts of entrants attend assessment centres in 1956, 1957, 1959 and 1960, and to help assess their potential a list of 25 personal attributes relevant to managerial success was developed. Follow-up checks showed that the assessment centre ratings were reasonable (but not overpowering) indicators of eventual management success. A surprise finding was that assessment centre methods were better predictors for non-college entrants to the organization than for graduates. This study is reported in D.W. Bray *et al. Formative Years in Business: A Long-Term AT & T Study of Managerial Lives* (Wiley, New York, 1974).

Aston Group A group of researchers at the University of Aston, Birmingham, England, in the approximate period 1962–70 and later. The key figures are Derek Pugh, David Hickson and Bob Hinings and in 'the second wave' John Child. The main points are that:

- The Aston Group is at the forefront of *contingency theory* (see separate entry).

- Their research embodies a vigorous approach to methodology and a concern with the specifics of measuring variable aspects of organizations.

- Their researchers demonstrated the pervasive influence of size as a determinant of organizational shape and structure.

- In particular they showed that some aspects of organization tend to 'cling together', namely specialization, standardization and formalism.

More generally the work of the Aston Group has shown that organizations may be more or less bureaucratic, and in terms of several different features. Previously, it had been presumed that Max Weber's concept of *bureaucracy* (see separate entry) described the real world.

Auditing Company law requires that every company should appoint a professionally qualified auditor. Many other types of enterprise are also subject to similar legal requirements. The basic role of the auditor is to make an independent examination of the accounts and underlying records. For this purpose the auditor has a legal right of access to the company's records, and an entitlement to full explanations from management. The normal audit report is a brief formal statement, so that any special comment from the auditor (commonly termed a 'qualification' of the audit report) stands out. Traditionally companies have tended to try to avoid any expression of reservation in the audit report, believing that readers of accounts would view these with concern, so that company auditors can have a substantial influence on the accounting practices adopted by management.

Professional accounting firms sell their clients a wide range of services besides auditing, ranging from accounting and tax advice to a whole host of consultancy activities. There is some controversy as to the extent to which the provision of these services undermines the independence which the auditor is supposed to possess.

Large organizations will often have an internal audit department, reporting to senior management on how the control systems of the enterprise are operating. Internal audit is not necessarily concerned exclusively with accounting issues. For example, a number of local authority internal audit departments employ engineers to check that energy conservation systems are operating properly.

'Social audit' is a term sometimes used to describe an independent investigation designed to consider whether an organization has given due consideration to its wider social responsibilities. Such investigations have sometimes been carried out at the request of management, but have more frequently been undertaken in opposition to the business. Critics argue that the term 'audit' applied to this kind of activity is misleading, giving a bogus impression of precision in the formulation of subjective judgements.

Aufsichtsrat The larger public companies in West Germany (those with AG after the name) have two-tier boards. The higher supervisory board, called the *Aufsichtsrat*, appoints and has veto power over the lower executive committee or *Vorstand*, which actually runs the company. The importance of this institution is that the German *Aufsichtsrat* is a practical solution to the problem of who will oversee top management, and dismiss them if they fail.

Authority   Usually defined as the ability to get others to do things, accept orders, implement instructions; it is usually differentiated from power by reason of its putative legitimacy, typically conferred by some position in a formal organization.

There are two main strands in the management literature on authority. The first is concerned to denote a variety of bases for authority, indicating that authority may derive from expert power or specialist knowledge, from charisma, moral stature or other personal qualities, as well as from occupancy of an office carrying authority in an organization. A variation on this theme is to note that office-based authority may be strengthened by (some of) these other bases. The second strand is a debate, in effect, about whether authority is contextually specific, i.e., limited to a particular situation, or is it more general, e.g., will the bank manager naturally rise to be captain of the sailing club, is it realistic for Americans to seek presidential candidates among business leaders and successful generals, and so on.

More critical for many managers, especially those who are new to the post, is the question of how to make authority effective – being branch manager is fine, but will anyone actually do what I say? A few tips may be given:

- At the beginning it helps a new incumbent of a position of authority to be 'anointed' by someone who already enjoys effective authority, to be brought in as such a person's successor, henchman or chosen agent.

- Circulate and talk to people, spread goodwill and learn some of the things you need to know which are not in the reports and computer print-outs.

- Get close to colleagues and subordinates so as to be able to influence them, lowering social barriers as a preliminary.

- Get people to accept orders incrementally, starting with the routine and uncontroversial; taking orders is habit forming.

- If an order is likely to evoke resistance, ask first those who are most likely to accept it; compliance is affected by the power of example.

- The compliance of subordinates will be affected by what *you* can do for *them* and how well you can do it: can you dispense information, answer questions, get people what they want, adjudicate, solve problems for subordinates; can you get them resources, co-operation from other people, sensible decisions from other managers, anything they need to be able to do their jobs?

B

Back-Selling A marketing tactic whereby one promotes not the raw material or input but products made or derived from it, in order to drive up demand for the input. The production connections are usually well recognized: that demand for glass, for instance, depends on the construction and automobile industries, but the promotional aspect is often neglected. Wood pulp, for example, does not lend itself to promotional advertising, but newspapers, Christmas cards and toilet rolls do.

Bad Debts When a business sells goods on credit terms it will sometimes prove impractical to obtain payment from the customer. Such losses are known as bad debts. The amount of bad debts that a business can afford depends on profit margins. For example, traditional bank lending on modest interest charges is very cautious, and a bank manager would expect to keep bad debts below 1% of lending. By contrast, credit card lending carries high interest charges and credit card companies have a corresponding willingness to take higher risks on lending.

See also *credit*.

Bakke, E. Wight An American academic who made a study of unemployment in the Great Depression of the 1930s. His books include *The Unemployed Man: A Social Study* (Nisbet & Co., London, 1933) and *Citizens Without Work* (Yale University Press, New Haven, 1940).

The study described in the first book is in fact of the unemployed in the Borough of Greenwich, London, using a naturalistic method of enquiry. Bakke boarded with a working-class family and over a period of months sought to develop easy relationships with the ordinary people of the borough, many of whom were unemployed.

His later study is a longitudinal team study of families where the traditional breadwinner was unemployed, in New Haven, Connecticut. Part of the interest of Bakke's work is that he is good at illuminating the differences between the American and British unemployed, capturing the deferential fatalism of the latter and contrasting it with the more proactive American response, where the victims of unemployment did not hesitate, for instance, to exploit their connections in grass roots political parties and make use of their contacts generally. Indeed Bakke's portrayal of the English working class ethos is quite masterly: he shows the public deference and fear of authority that older age groups in Britain still exhibit.

In the New Haven study Bakke is good at depicting the stages of deprivation – reaction to the unemployed experience – as well as tracing the effects of unemployment on family integration over time by means of some quite fascinating family case studies. Indeed, although unemployment in general is socially destructive, a few of the families were brought together by the effort to mitigate its rigours.

Citizens Without Work is actually a mine of both practical and psychological tips for surviving unemployment. Bakke's work in general should be compulsory reading for those who engage in the thoughtless dismemberment of companies.

Balance Sheet An accounting statement which is drawn up periodically (normally once a year). It shows the assets owned by the business, the liabilities owed by the business and the difference between the two, which is referred to as the owners' *equity*. Thus the balance sheet equation can be summarized simply as:

$$\text{Assets} - \text{Liabilities} = \text{Equity}$$

There are two broad types of asset. Fixed assets are held for long-term use in the business, including items such as property, plant and vehicles. Current assets are held for the short term (normally defined as one year), and include items such as stock, debtors and cash.

Liabilities similarly are normally divided into long-term items (over one year to the payment date) and current items (under one year). The difference between assets and liabilities is often called the *net assets*.

The equity side of the balance sheet shows the history of how the proprietors' interest in the business has been accumulated. In a UK limited company the equity will be analysed into three broad headings:

(a)   *The nominal value* of share capital, representing the amount shareholders have subscribed for the nominal value of their shares.

(b)   *Capital reserves*, being the total surpluses accumulated for shareholders other than by earning realized profits. Examples are the 'share premium' reserve, which represents any amount paid into the company for shares in excess of their nominal value, and the 'Revaluation' reserve, representing any surplus on revaluation.

(c)   *Revenue reserves*, being total realized profits accumulated by the company which have not yet been paid out as dividends. A company is not allowed to pay any dividend in excess of the revenue reserves.

The term 'reserve' does not represent a hoard of resources, as in everyday language, but is simply a historical record of how the equity has been accumulated.

It is important to be aware that a balance sheet does *not* show what a business is 'worth'. There are two reasons for this:

(a)   Individual assets and liabilities are not all shown at their current value. Some, if not all, will be shown at their historical cost or at an out-of-date valuation.

(b)   A business as a whole generally has a very different value from the total value of individual assets and liabilities. This difference, known as 'goodwill', arises because of the various connections a business accumulates in the course of trading.

Bank   The major banks each provide a fairly standard range of services to business. Thus managers are often surprised to learn how different branches, even of the same bank, may respond to customer requests in different ways. As an example, we know a large town where new small business initiatives have been attracted by a number of well-designed incentives. The result is that local banks are very selective in choosing projects to finance because of the wide range of choice they enjoy. An astute local accountant guides his clients to the banks in a nearby market town, where far fewer such applications are received so that those bank branches are keen to do business.

Bargaining   Bargaining affects the manager in a whole host of situations, both explicit and implicit. Obvious examples are collective bargaining with employees (see *industrial relations*) and agreements between buyer and seller (see *buying power*). Less obvious are bargains struck to facilitate working within the organization. Here the explicit bargain, e.g., 'If you get this printed by Thursday, I will support your claims in the budget committee', is less common than an implicit offering of future support, e.g., 'Be a pal and . . .'. Whether explicit or implicit such 'bargains' tend to build up relationships that affect the way an organization works.

Barnard, C.I.   Chester Barnard was president of the New Jersey Bell Telephone Company but is best known as the author of one of the early theoretical books about management, *Functions of the Executive*, first published in 1938. In this original and challenging book Barnard makes out a case for the study of management, and analyses the factors involved in co-operation; he originates the concepts of effectiveness and efficiency and distinguishes between them, using in this enterprise what later came to be called the notion of latent function (the idea that actions have unintended and sometimes undesirable effects). Barnard defines the formal organization, and develops an equilibrium concept of the organization. At the same time he distinguishes between formal and informal organization, and is good at working out the ways in which the informal may sustain and supplement the formal. His work also embraces a typology of bases for specialization, a theory of authority and a theory of motivation and incentives, as well as a preliminary analysis of decision-making.

   Functions of the Executive does not make easy reading: the ideas which it handles are genuinely difficult (and the style is sometimes ponderous). But it is an impressive theoretical achievement; part of its strength and fascination is a repeated 'going back to square one' and asking – and answering – questions such as how do organizations arise, why do people serve in them, what motivates, how is division of labour arranged, and why are orders (mostly) obeyed?

Batch Production   Batch production refers to the manufacture of an item in 'reasonable numbers'. In the scale uniqueness–standardization it comes above unit production, i.e., making single items, or jobbing, i.e., finding customers

14

who want one or two of something made, and below fully standardized mass production. Arguably most demanding for management, batch production needs balance between versatility/flexibility and scale economies/control.

Benefits   Employee benefits cover all kinds of goods and services provided by the business in addition to monetary remuneration. They can be linked to the work of the enterprise in two ways:

(a)   Those provided to be used for business purposes or to improve work performance. For example, many companies provide highly subsidized and attractive dining facilities as an inducement to keep employees on the premises at lunch time, thereby cutting down on the length of lunch-break taken and also on lunch-time drinking.

(b)   Benefits provided which are samples of the product of the enterprise. One of the most widely envied is the low interest mortgage provided for employees by most financial institutions.

Some benefits which seem highly extravagant in the USA or the UK might be common in some overseas appointments. For example, a chauffeur-driven car is a common benefit provided by multinationals to expatriate managers working in countries where a foreigner in a traffic accident is likely to be treated severely.

Benefits may be an especially attractive form of employee remuneration when tax rates are high. Consequently, tax authorities in most countries tend to try to identify and quantify such benefits. Such a process is necessarily crude in its application, so that many benefits continue to be effectively tax-free while some may actually be rendered undesirable by the tax system.

Black Box   The situation where a process is so technically complex that the user cannot understand how it operates. The solution is to regard the process as a 'black box' which cannot be penetrated, and simply to accept the output. Thus the manager delegates all handling of the process to a technical expert. The concept has particular value when applied to the use of a computer, which allows managers to enjoy the benefit of the computer's capacity to handle a mass of data without having to understand the technicalities of how the machine works.

The danger of a 'black box' approach is that it can become an excuse for failure to control activities for which the manager is responsible.

Blake's Grid   Robert Blake together with Jane Mouton developed the famous management grid for grading supervisors and managers in the two dimensions of concern for task and concern for people, both on a 1–9 scale where 9 is top (R.R. Blake and J.S. Mouton, *The Management Grid*, Gulf Publisher, Houston, 1964). Knowledge of the grid is widespread, and this is reflected in what have become common phrases in the vocabulary of managers, such as 'he's a 9.1 man', strong on task and doesn't care about people, or 'country club

15

management', strong social skills and people oriented but weak on task accomplishment.

An interesting sidelight on the meaning of these two grid dimensions is provided by a later study by two other Americans, Jay Hall and Susan Donnell. They graded a sample of 12,000 managers as successful, average or below average in terms of career and performance, and they administered various tests, including Blake's grid. As one might expect the successful managers scored high on both dimensions, the below average low on both, but the surprise comes in the middle: the average performers tended to be good on task but not so good on people. Put more pungently, taking the job seriously will get you from poor to average, but you need people skills to get from average to good. (Jay Hall and Susan Donnell, 'Managerial achievement: the personal side of behavioural theory', *Human Relations* **32** (1).)

Board of Directors The body legally charged with running the company in the interests of the shareholders. In a country such as Britain which only has one board as opposed to the two-tier board system in several of the continental countries (see *Aufsichtsrat* for a German comparison) the board of directors is *the* policy-making body. The typical board is made up of functional bosses (heads of sales, production, finance and so on) presided over by a managing director, and a critical question for the quality of the board's deliberation is the ability of individual directors to see beyond the interests of the department they head up.

There are one or two anomalies associated with the British board of directors. One is that the relevant legislation allows for the appointment of both *executive* and *non-executive directors* (see separate entries) and there is a variable mix thereof from company to company. Another is that the managing director may also be chairman of the board, and this arrangement is common, though contemporary opinion regards this as undesirable in that a separate chairman would be better able to exercise a watchdog function.

The board of directors also offers clues as to the values of the business in terms of what functions and interests are represented. One can also perceive national level contrasts here with, for instance, an over-representation of design and production in West Germany.

Book Value The amount at which an asset is recorded in the accounts. Because of the artificiality of accounting conventions it does not necessarily bear any relationship to the real value of the asset (see *balance sheet*). For example, we know a small business with a property valued at £250,000 which shows that property in the accounts at a precise figure of £3,113 – because that was the cost when the business was founded back in 1890!

Borrowing Powers Most limited companies contain a clause in their documents of incorporation limiting the total amount they are allowed to borrow, called their 'borrowing powers'. This is normally computed as a multiple of the share capital and reserves (see *Balance sheet*).

Loan agreements often include similar restrictions, but sometimes involve a tighter commitment to restrict borrowing. In the USA such limitations are termed 'debt covenants'.

Boston Consulting Group (BCG) Source of a widely quoted theory of how an enterprise should regard its mix of investments. For each type of product they ask two questions:

(a) What is the product growth rate?

(b) What is the company's share of the market?

A simple matrix shows that each product must fall under one of four headings:

	Share of market	
	High	**Low**
High Product Growth rate	Stars (a)	Problem children (c)
Low	Cash cows (b)	Dogs (d)

Taking each in turn:

(a) Stars are highly promising. With a high share of the market the company should enjoy good economies of scale and therefore earn high profits. To expand fast enough to keep up with high market growth cash resources need to be allocated to developing these products.

(b) Cash cows should also be profitable because of the high market share. In view of the low growth rate there should be little need for new investment, so that cash flows from these profits can be diverted to other parts of the business.

(c) Problem children are a dilemma. Low market share is unsatisfactory, since the company cannot compete successfully with others enjoying economies of scale. At the same time the high product growth rate offers a tempting opportunity. The BCG theory is that the company should make a clear-cut decision either to drop such a product or to pour in sufficient resources to boost market share.

(d) Dogs are unprofitable because of low market share and unpromising in view of the low growth rate. The BCG theory is that such products should be dropped.

The BCG theory has to be applied with some care. We know a consultant who was asked to advise a company on how to dispose of a division regarded as a 'dog'. On investigation he found that the division was in fact highly profitable – management had failed to realize that this product was highly successful within a particular section of its overall market.

Boundary In *socio-technical systems theory* (see separate entry) 'boundary' refers to the interface between the organization and its environment and to the interface between the parts making up the system. It may be important to focus on these boundaries, especially the internal ones, to see what exchanges (inputs and outputs) are being made across the boundary lines.

Brainstorming A conference technique whereby a group tries to solve a specific problem by collecting together all the ideas spontaneously contributed by its members. The exercise involves two stages:

(a) First, all participants are given a problem and are asked to put forward in discussion any ideas which come to mind. They are encouraged to make their suggestions without regard to how apparently far-fetched they may seem.

(b) At the second stage all suggestions are analysed. These are then evaluated so that an agreed practical solution emerges.

Brainstorming is most commonly used as an educational technique to promote both group involvement and creativity. It can also be used by a management team seeking a new approach to a problem.

Brand Loyalty/Brand Change Brand loyalty is of the utmost importance in the domain of *fast-moving consumer goods* (see separate entry) and much advertising is aimed at sustaining this loyalty/getting consumers to change preference. So the key question is: what makes people change?

David Ogilvy and Joel Raphaelson writing in the *Harvard Business Review* ('Research on advertising techniques that work – and don't work', July–August 1982, pp. 14–18) identify seven (advertising) factors likely to instigate brand change:

(a) The advertised item *solves a real problem;* the consumer cannot start his car on cold mornings but this product will make it happen.

(b) Using *humour,* but only where humour is acceptable; you can make jokes about people's choice of holiday but not about the provision of funeral services.

(c) *Public figures* used in adverts must be *relevant* to the product or service; a film star can promote fur coats but not DIY kits.

(d) *'Real-life' interviews* in which someone committed to the product convinces someone who is not.

(e) Clips showing the *product or service in action*, when 'it does not know' it is being watched.

(f) Conventional *demonstrations* of quality or efficacy of product.

(g) *News*: advert includes a genuine news element, in that, for instance, the product really is new/did not exist before, or incorporates a new technology or operating principle.

What is more, Ogilvy and Raphaelson show that those who change brands buy more of the new brand than those who do not change buy of the old brand.

Bretton Woods The Bretton Woods Conference in 1944 formulated an international agreement setting up the *International Monetary Fund* (see separate entry) and establishing a system for managing fixed exchange rates. This system was relaxed under the Smithsonian Agreement of 1971 and generally abandoned, in favour of floating exchange rates, by 1973.

Many managers would prefer a system of fixed exchange rates because this would remove one element of uncertainty in international trade. The European Monetary System offers a system for minimizing exchange rate fluctuations in the European Community but the UK has not yet joined this arrangement.

Bridlington Agreement Laid down by the *Trades Union Congress* (see separate entry) in 1939, the Bridlington Agreement lays down a set of rules designed to prevent trade unions from poaching members from each other. The agreement does *not* offer a mechanism for the rationalization of union jurisdiction.

Budget A formal statement of the planned allocation of financial resources for a future period of time. An overall budget (often called the 'master budget') will summarize the total plan for the enterprise while individual budgets will cover separate aspects of the business plan in detail. An example of the latter is the 'cash budget' which looks at the impact of the planned operations on the cash resources of the business.

In drawing up a budget it is necessary to co-ordinate data from all the management functions. Often this is done by setting up a 'budget committee' with representatives from each department of the business. It is important that managers are aware that budgets present, in financial terms, plans which they themselves have participated in preparing.

See also *zero-based budgeting*.

Bureaucracy Those who seek a rational rather than emotional definition of bureaucracy usually start with the formulation of Max Weber, the late nineteenth–early twentieth century economic historian and sociologist. Weber's view is that bureaucratic organization is marked by:

19

- a hierarchy of authority
- division of labour among employees
- employment of technically competent officials
- procedures for accomplishing tasks
- rules governing behaviour of officials
- limited authority of office
- differential rewards by office
- the separation of administration from ownership
- an emphasis on written communication
- rationality.

Weber, of course, was seeking to characterize civil administrative organizations rather than business enterprises, but it is still reasonable to ask: Is the business firm a bureaucracy?

Clearly, all firms are bureaucracies to some extent. They have some of the above features, even if the degree varies. At the same time, business firms are differentiated by their striving to make a profit, and their ethos is different too, stressing ingenuity and achievement rather than impersonal and impartial administration.

It is this last consideration which is the clue to explain the fact that bureaucracy has come to be a dirty word. While some of the features of bureaucracy outlined above are indispensable for the conduct of business, and bureaucracy in general represents a cost-effective means for dealing with routine, it is the *ethos* of bureaucracy which is anathema to business. Bureaucracy goes with stability, routine, predictability and rectitude, when companies need to compete, change, innovate, respond to the market and think big.

So, the message is that bureaucratic methods may be fine for processing the routine, but bureaucratic thinking is death to proactivity and flexibility.

Bureaugenic   Tending to induce bureaucracy, and therefore not desirable.

Burnham, James   See *managerial revolution*.

Burns, T.   Tom Burns, retired professor of sociology from the University of Edinburgh, is best known for a book he published with G.M. Stalker, *The Management of Innovation* (Tavistock Press, London, 1961). Based primarily on a sample of British companies which are moving into the electronic industry in the 1950s, the authors argue that there are two ideal-type organizational structures, the *mechanistic* and the *organic*. The mechanistic is marked by clear-cut lines of authority and communication, tasks are clearly specified, the direction of communication is upward–downward, and indeed the organization is quite formally structured. This mechanistic structure, say Burns and Stalker, is appropriate to companies operating in conditions of stability. It contrasts with the organic structure marked by unclear task specification, attenuated hierarchy, and above all by a plenitude of lateral and diagonal communications. In contrast to the mechanistic structure, in which rank determines status, individual status in the organic structure is a reflection of the special knowledge and experience that people have, and their value to the mission. This organic structure is appropriate to companies facing change, whether in the form of new markets or the mastery of new technology.

These ideas have been influential. They have served as a charter for 'freeing-up' organizations which faced the challenge of major change, as well as for having a more liberal régime in the R & D milieu. It should be added that as an organization moves from conditions of stability into a change situation, it does not automatically develop from mechanistic to organic; such a transition may be impeded by the status and political systems or even by the individual chief executive should he feel threatened by the ambiguities of the organic structure. Burns and Stalker's argument is rather that the transition *ought* to occur, and would serve the end of adjusting to change successfully.

Burns and Stalker are part of a wider movement in the literature on organizations, on both sides of the Atlantic. The basic message is that organization structure is not invariable, not always and everywhere the same, and may vary with technology, type of goal, strategy and needs for integration, as well as on the stability–change dimension.

Business Expansion Scheme (BES) This scheme allows investors who subscribe for new shares in a small business to claim tax relief on their investment, provided they are not managers or employees of the business. Those interested in such an investment can arrange to invest either directly in such businesses or through a 'portfolio' organized by a financial institution, so spreading their risk.

Business Policy Term sometimes used to describe the broad area of *corporate strategy* (see separate entry).

Buying Power The relative power of buyers and sellers when bargaining depends on a wide range of factors. Buyers are particularly powerful when:

- The buyer purchases in large volume. This is particularly the case where the supplier carries high fixed costs, and so will suffer severe loss from a major decline in sales.

- The product purchased is a standard one that can be bought from a range of suppliers.

- The buyer can credibly threaten to manufacture the goods as an alternative to purchase. We know a food manufacturing company which

21

deliberately produce some of their own packaging materials as a bargaining point with suppliers of bought-in packaging materials.

- Quality of the product is easily assessed.

Suppliers are powerful when:

- Their industry is concentrated in a few companies selling to a wide range of customers.

- The product has built up *switching costs* (see separate entry) so that buyers face costs in switching suppliers.

- The product is unique in some way.

- It is difficult for customers to meet their requirements by substitution of an alternative product.

Power in the hands of buyers and suppliers is often reflected in other ways than selling prices. For example, we know a major retail chain that 'punishes' late deliveries by withholding orders from the offending supplier for a period, an effective sanction because of their buying power.

Abuse of power on either side of the buyer/seller relationship can be damaging, in the long run, to both parties. For example, many local councils are known to pay contractors slowly and as a result do not receive tenders from small firms which might well prove substantially cheaper.

C

Call-Off A lot of industrial buyer–seller relations are in terms of rolling, incremental deliveries by the supplier-seller to the user-buyer rather than discrete orders. Thus the engineering firm consumes millions of screws in a year, and the chain retailer sells thousands of pairs of socks a month, and both have running contracts with suppliers not one-off orders. And the number per time period which the buyer takes is the call-off rate, and buyers typically vary the call-off rate to suit their needs. Variable call-off rates tend to lead to closer buyer–seller relations (see *quasi-vertical integration*), and to require better management/work organization on the side of the supplier.

Capital A term used by accountants, confusingly, in a variety of ways.

The term 'capital' can be used to indicate the equity in the business, i.e., the owner's investment. The term is widely used in this sense in the accounts of unincorporated businesses. In a limited company equity consists of 'share capital' plus 'reserves' (see *balance sheet*).

In a broader sense the term 'capital' is often used to describe all the long-term financial resources of the business, both equity and long-term loans ('loan capital'). 'Capital employed' may comprise either of these first two definitions, or may also include short-term borrowings as well.

A 'capital' asset is one which is held for the long term. When an item is recorded as a fixed asset in the balance sheet it is said to be 'capitalized', and any purchase of new fixed assets is termed 'capital expenditure'.

Managers should never feel embarrassed to ask any accountant who uses the word 'capital' to define the term more closely.

See also *balance sheet, working capital.*

Careers   Most managers and professionals want a career as well as remuneration; they wish, that is, to move through a succession of graded posts to achieve some organizational position and influence and to enjoy an enhancement of status.

This fact is recognized by many companies in their establishment of management development departments, which counsel, plan and facilitate careers, attempting to get a fit between the expectations of the individual and the realities of the organization, between the strengths of the individual and the needs of the company.

The point to emphasize is that the career expectation is part of the manager's set of presenting demands. Not only is the manager looking for the advancement itself, but more widely for things thought to be associated with it in the middle term – training, exposure, responsibility, the chance to innovate, control and motivate, and so on. And these properties of jobs are part of the sacrifice and reward package: they can be balanced against downside features.

Finally, personnel organizers in multinationals often presume that Anglo-Saxon careerist norms apply equally everywhere. They do not, even among the richer industrial nations. Salary compression (Portugal), high marginal taxation (Scandinavia), great respect for intellectual attainment (France) or, say, an anti-individualistic national culture (Netherlands) may all effect/modify attitudes to careers and promotion.

Carlson, Sune   Now retired Swedish economics professor from the University of Uppsala, famous for the first ever study of what it is that senior managers 'do all day'. Carlson made a study of nine Swedish managing directors using the activity diary method, and wrote up the findings in *Executive Behaviour* (Strömbergs, Stockholm, 1951). The principal interest of this pioneering study is that it seriously modifies the (formerly) popular conception of the detached Olympian chief executive, devoted to longer term strategy formulation. Carlson's managing directors, in fact, were hardly ever alone, had pressurized and fragmented work patterns, and were much more deeply involved in short-term and fire-fighting activities than anyone had ever supposed. They worked long hours but deceived themselves about it, failed to delegate, and treated as temporary states of affairs which to Carlson seemed permanent. Horrified by these departures from good management, Carlson coined the phrase 'administrative pathology' to designate the situation in which the manager recognizes that what he is doing is wrong, but seems powerless to correct the trend. In particular Carlson highlights the vicious circle whereby top managers are too often interrupted to have time to develop policies, but if they did have time to develop them, they would provide guidance for colleagues who endlessly interrupt them seeking rulings on particular cases.

Case Study   The case study is one of the most commonly used methods of management teaching. Harvard Business School has led the way in developing this approach. A case is an account of a business situation, real or imaginary. Normally a case is presented in written form, but video or computer software material may also be used. The content of the case will be designed to highlight certain aspects of a situation.

The instructor presents the material to a group of students, and conducts a discussion of the case. The instructor's role is to guide the group with carefully designed questions to draw out the major issues. Another approach is to open the case discussion by presenting a number of alternative solutions. Benefits of this training method include:

- Students can learn from 'real life' situations. Harvard cases, for example, are all based on actual situations.

- A case can show how a set of facts can be interpreted in a variety of ways.

- The case study, being based on 'realistic' problems, prompts a practical approach both by student and teacher.

- The variety of interpretations highlighted by a good case leads participants away from the view that every problem has a single 'correct' solution.

Cash Cow   Term used by the *Boston Consulting Group* (see separate entry) to describe a product with a high market share but low growth rate. It is argued that these products offer little scope for growth, and so should yield substantial cash flows for the rest of the business.

Cash Flow   To survive a business must be able to meet its liabilities as they fall due. In simple terms, the business must be able to pay the wages at the end of the week.

Trading cash flows arise because cash flows in from the customers of the business and flows out to those who supply goods, services and labour. If the business is trading profitably then in the long term the firm will enjoy net cash inflows. However, a firm which is expanding rapidly may find that, in the short term, large amounts of cash are tied up in holding increased stock and in extending trade credit to the increased number of customers. If management has not planned for this increased cash requirement then they may be unable to pay amounts owing, and actually go bankrupt as a result of increasing profits!

The moral is that management must, when considering any financial decision, plan *both* for profitability and to ensure that the cash resources of the business are adequate.

Centralization   Centralization is currently out of favour, the prevailing view being that decentralization (see separate entry) will increase flexibility (it will) and develop decision-making skills and commitment among more junior managers (probably).

The case for centralization is this:

- it is good for control;

- it is good for getting the most out of economies of scale (central sourcing, specialized production centres, and so on);

- it is associated with success in retailing (see *retail operations*);

- it is a natural response when the organization is threatened or in turn-round situations.

There is no golden rule − it depends on what you want most: control, direction, economies and implementation of strategic plans, or adaptability, speed of response and innovation.

Chain of Command   The set of authority positions on a vertical line. In theory, orders and exhortations pass down it, and information passes up it. While celebrated in the classical management literature, the modern view is that it is best to keep the chain of command short, and to delegate discretion downwards to those closest to the operating exigencies. See also *authority* and *classical management*.

Chandler, Alfred   American business historian with whom two key ideas are associated. The first is that the laws of the free market derived from theoretical economics do not work in practice because of the size, power and wilfulness of major corporations. These fix prices, strive for monopoly, achieve market dominance in some cases, and use financial and marketing clout to create demand and move products. This idea is not fashionable any more (see *naked market*). It says more about the 1960s than the 1980s, but the day may come again.

The second idea is the formulation that structure follows strategy, that, to cite Chandler's inspiration as example, companies pursuing strategies of diversification and multinational expansion will tend to move from a functional to a divisional structure.

Change   The need for change confronts most business organizations most of the time − gradually, intermittently, sometimes dramatically. The principal reasons are:

- technology change, making new products, services or methods possible and desirable

- a tendency for most products to have a limited life, such that piecemeal adoption of a new product is followed by a mature phase of expanding, then steady sales followed in turn by a declining phase (the product life cycle theory of marketing specialists)

- competition
- other changes in the environment, affecting such things as taste, need, consumer demands, as well as employee aspirations and career expectations

Thus the need to fashion a response to change is always with us.

Both the academic literature and the popular view postulate a strong link between change and creativity, and this is quite right. In consequence, it is difficult to formulate rules for change: recognizing the need for change, and working out what that change should be, is largely a matter of intuitive judgement and situational imagination. Having said this, the organization of change may well call for detailed and integrated staff work of a very rational kind. A judgement in favour of making an existing product from a new material, for example, may involve new sourcing, tooling and operating procedures, some changes in the workforce mix and related supervisory practices, together with modifications to the distribution system and a new advertising campaign: all this needs to be planned and co-ordinated. Or to put it another way, the origination of change and its implementation are qualitatively different tasks and require different manager skills.

There are clearly obstacles to change, even when such change is manifestly desirable. Apart from tradition and inertia, powerful individuals in an organization may obstruct change if they feel threatened by it. It is also clear that the readiness or otherwise to change – to test reality, posit alternatives, experiment and implement – is a variable aspect of corporate culture. Some cultures lend themselves to change while others do not; in other words to manage change may mean to modify corporate culture.

But most important for the implementation of change is the commitment of rank and file organizational members. Bland assurances will be counterproductive. Employees need intelligible information, support and empathy, in particular support to help them develop new skills, perhaps even skills of dealing with new people as colleagues or supervisors; they may also need support in solving technical operating problems, or enhanced access to people who can help with this. And it also helps to give employees as much control over the rate of personal learning as is practicable.

Chargehand   In the typical British factory, the chargehand is a production worker who exercises a minor supervisory function at the same time, usually over other workers in the group to which he belongs. The chargehand is thus distinct from the foreman, or first-line supervisor, who does not work alongside the men but has a full-time supervisory function.

Chief Executive   Refers to the American style chief executive officer (CEO), or highest full-time manager in a company, responsible to the shareholders' representatives for company performance, equivalent to the managing director in Britain. The term is widely used in Britain as well, although the legal phraseology is different.

Classical Management   A movement for the codification of the principles of management and administration which started with the writings of the French mining engineer Henri Fayol around the First World War and held sway into the 1950s and 1960s when, principally, sociologists investigated business firms and undermined the principles by showing that there are more differences and relativities than had been expected.

The essence of classical management is the formulation of principles of management presumed to have universal applicability, i.e., be always true and relevant to companies, even formal organizations of all types. These include precepts such as:

- *unity of command*: an organizational member should not receive orders from more than one superior;

- *exception principle*: decisions which recur frequently should be reduced to a routine and delegated to subordinates with only the non-recurring decisions handled by superiors;

- *span of control*: keep it within bounds to maintain the real supervisory control of managers;

- *unity of objectives*: the objectives of each part of the organization should be harmonized and integrated to achieve overall organizational goals;

- *authority and responsibility*: these should be clearly defined for organizational members, and should balance; people must have the authority to execute that for which they are responsible.

The importance of the movement is two-fold. First, it constitutes an original attempt to say what management is all about, to provide a functional analysis of the means and ends of management. Second, most of the precepts are still seen as having a fundamental rightness, even if they have been supplemented and relativized. After Henri Fayol, the principal exponents of the movement are Luther Gulick in the USA (member of President Roosevelt's administrative management committee in the 1930s) and Lyndale Urwick in Britain (co-founder of the famous consultancy firm).

Some accounts lump scientific management and classical management together but this is wrong: the former deals with the rationalization of blue-collar work and wage incentives, the latter with general principles of management aimed at 'getting it right'. See *scientific management* and *Fayol*.

Close   A close is the manner in which a sale is closed. Because of a natural human reluctance to take decisions, thereby excluding other options and perhaps making mistakes, even people who 'really' want to buy what is on offer may vacillate at the point of decision. To counter this salesmen have developed a number of contrived moves (closes) to bring people to say yes/sign the order form. See, for example, *puppy-dog close*.

Close Company   This term is used in UK tax law to describe a situation where a company is under the control of a small number of shareholders. The main significance of such a classification is that the Inland Revenue may force the company to pay part of its profits out as dividend, so that income tax has to be paid by the individual recipients. There are very detailed tax rules to identify such a situation and quantify the dividend to be paid. During the 1980s the close company rules have been substantially relaxed and personal tax rates have fallen, reducing the impact on business of this legislation.

Closed System   In *socio-technical systems theory* (see separate entry) a closed system is one where the interdependent parts affect each other (a change in one part is followed by a change in another) but the whole is shut off from its environment. See also *open system*.

Common Stock   US term for ordinary shares (see *shares*).

Communications   The trouble with research on communications is that it is stronger on problems than solutions. So, one service which can be provided for managers is to relativize the issue; another is to indicate where difficulties are likely to be encountered.

Communications became a fetish in the post-war growth period, the assumption being that if you get communications right, everything else will be fine. Management and workers do have different interests at many points, and good communications won't make the differences disappear. If the order book is thin, and you have to make people redundant, they will hate it no matter how nicely you tell them.

Similarly, there are differences of interest between the various functions. Communications between sales and production may well be poor, but that is an effect, not a cause, of their different interests and capacities.

But where are communications problems most likely? First, there is a well-known tendency for downward communication to become garbled. There is no known cure, but some counter-measures include keeping the lines short, checking sometimes what is coming out at the bottom, and expecting it to happen. Second, communications upward tend to be deliberately distorted to offer a pleasing account to those higher up; again, expect it, go and have a look for yourself, ask different people and if you think something is being concealed, ask the question in a way that makes admission easier. Third, communication between manager and immediate boss is often poor, with the manager colouring statements to influence the boss, and the boss's communications being misapprehended or neutralized as unacceptable. It is part of the wider tension of the superior–subordinate relationship; one can simply try to build trust and openness, but it cannot be done overnight.

There is some good news:

- Not only do managers generally prefer face-to-face communication rather than written, it is also more effective in changing attitudes and behaviour.

- Most organizations generate and circulate too much information; you can probably reduce the overload without impairing the ends of good communication.

- Employees, especially at lower levels, are much influenced by unofficial communications – by the comments of work-group members, chance remarks of third parties, their observation of what is happening – as well as by official feedback; try to make some of this work for you.

Remember that actions speak louder than words. It is no good saying, 'This company's greatest asset is people' if you have just put 300 of them in the dole queue.

Company   In the UK there are two types of limited company:

(a)   Public companies, having the letters 'Plc' after their name. Such companies are subject to some expensive and onerous legal obligations but enjoy the right to offer their securities for sale to the general public.

(b)   Private companies, having the letters 'Ltd' after their name. Such companies have less expensive formalities to comply with compared to Plcs, but are not allowed to issue securities to the general public.

Company Cars   The exquisite popularity of company cars in Britain often excites international comment. In general terms this British penchant for fringe benefits reflects management salaries that are uncompetitive by international standards, but there is also a particular tax advantage. While the company car is taxed at the same percentage rate a salary increment would be, it is not the whole value of the car that is so taxed, just a much smaller sum deemed the 'taxable benefit'.

Company Law   In western economies the most common form of business enterprise is the limited liability company. Each country has its own code of company law defining the roles and responsibilities of directors and other managers. A manager moving to a country where he has no previous experience would well be advised to check out what responsibilities he carries under local company law.
   See also *limited liability*.

Comparative Management   This is a study of management style in different countries. It focuses on the interesting differences, the strengths and weaknesses and relates them to the wider society and culture.
   It is important because differences do exist, but they tend to be culturally

embedded differences which take some getting at. Businessmen often have only a superficial knowledge of the countries they deal with, gleanings from the airport lounge and the hotel bar. Looking systematically at management in another country also provides a comparison for your own country and a sense of what it is like.

Compensation   Compensation is the polite term for the monetary reward for doing work. It is probably fair to say that financial rewards have been considerably underplayed by social scientists from the time of the Hawthorne studies onwards (see *human relations*).

The case for financial rewards, however, has now been (re)established by an excellent study reviewing the research/literature on employee performance of four things:

(a)   participation, or employee involvement in decision-making

(b)   goal-setting, that is assigning specific and challenging goals as against easy 'do your best' goals

(c)   job enrichment, instilling greater variety, responsibility and challenge

(d)   money, the employment of pay incentive schemes

The top two, from the number of studies reviewed showing a positive connection between the potential motivator and actual gains in performance, were money and goal-setting. That is, every piece of research reviewed showed enhanced money rewards and goal-setting to lead to better performance, as opposed to 92% of the studies on job enrichment and performance and only half of the studies of participation and performance. (See E.A. Locke *et al.* 'The relative effectiveness of four methods of motivating employee performance' in K.D. Duncan *et al.* (eds) *Changes in Working Life*, Wiley, Chichester, 1980.)

Recent research, in fact, suggests that if there is one motivator more powerful than money it is an enhanced pay system which employees have helped to design.

Competitive Advantage   When a business is considering the development of new products it is said to have a 'competitive advantage' in those areas closest to its core product. This is because of existing strengths both in production technology and marketing.

To take an example, a company with a long established record of manufacturing men's razors and razor blades moved into the production of women's razors and men's shaving cream. In the case of the women's razors they moved away from their traditional market but possessed competitive advantage in terms of production skills. Conversely in the shaving cream case they possessed strong existing marketing links and developed a new area of production technology.

Complex Man   The American psychologist Edgar Schein originated the concept of complex man in motivation theory. In part he has taken on board the (motivational) messages from various schools of thought – scientific management, human relations, neo-human relations – and combined and distilled them. Schein's understanding of complex man includes the following propositions:

- People are complex and highly variable. They have many motives which are arranged in some sort of hierarchy which is specific to the individual, and the hierarchy itself may change over time and between situations.

- People may acquire new objectives and alter their priorities as a result of organizational experiences.

- People may satisfy different needs in different life spheres, for example, security needs may be satisfied at work, social needs at home, and self-fulfilment needs in some leisure pursuit or voluntary activity (see *Maslow's need hierarchy*).

- People may respond to a variety of supervisory styles and management strategies depending on their (changing) priorities and circumstances. Thus there is no style or approach which is right for everyone all of the time.

The complex man model clearly has two practical implications for managers and especially supervisors. They need (to acquire) diagnostic ability, to know what is required. And they need flexibility in operating a repertoire of social skills and situational responses.

Concentration   Industrial concentration is the extent to which manufactured output is concentrated in a relatively small number of large firms, and one may make comparisons between countries in these terms. Thus the USA has a higher industrial concentration than West Germany, which in turn has a higher level than France.

One can also compare levels of concentration for particular sectors, both within and between countries. Thus, for instance, the overall level of concentration for Great Britain and West Germany is about the same, but there are some differences in sector values: higher concentration in the food, drink and tobacco industries in Britain, higher concentration in the chemical industry in Germany.

Concentration, whether national or sectional, is generally held to confer a competitive advantage. But it is probably not as simple as this, and the questions to ask are:

- Does this concentration facilitate economies of scale (or was the cut-off point past long ago)?

- Does it allow the R & D (research and development) spend to reach critical mass?

31

- Does it facilitate market dominance?

And if the answer to all these is yes, one should then query whether this concentration-determined advantage facilitates the exploitation of soft domestic markets as in the British food and drink example above, or strengthens the industry in tougher, international markets, as in the case of German chemicals.

Confederation of British Industry The CBI is an association of the managements of a wide variety of UK enterprises. It includes individual companies, a number of trade associations (including the National Farmers' Union), and several nationalized industries.

The basic functions of the CBI are to formulate and articulate a view on the policies needed to promote commerce and industry. The CBI has a full-time Director General who is widely quoted as representing the views of the UK business community.

Consignment Stocking This is a method which solves the problem of the availability of supplies for some manufacturers. It is an arrangement where the supplier provides a large quantity of a commodity on the premises of the buyer/user, who pays for small quantities as and when they are used. This gives the buyer continuity of supply/instant availability and low stock costs, while the supplier gets free warehousing on the buyer's premises and a nice even production throughput. In practice consignment stocking is only common in petrol, oil, bulk-containerized fluids, industrial gases and some chemicals in fluid or powder form. But in principle the method could be extended to other commodities; hard-pressed manufacturers worried about availability of inputs for the manufacturing programme might explore this option.

Consolidated Accounts When one company, known as the holding company, owns more than half the voting shares in another company, known as the subsidiary, then it effectively controls the activities of the investee. In these circumstances the holding company must normally present 'consolidated accounts' which include the assets, liabilities and profits or losses of the companies it controls. These accounts will also include the profits or losses, but not assets or liabilities, of 'associates', being companies where the holding company has a substantial and influential, but not controlling, shareholding.

Consolidated accounts aim to give a picture of a group of companies as a single economic entity. However, in law each company in a group is a separate legal entity responsible for its own obligations. For example, if you enter into a contract with a subsidiary company you cannot normally, in the event of default, make any claim against the holding company. Thus users of accounts may need to look in detail at accounts for an individual company, as well as the consolidated accounts.

Consultants   Management consultants are available covering the whole range of skills needed by an organization, and come from a range of backgrounds from the sole practitioner to large firms. The old joke that a consultant is 'someone who borrows your watch to tell you the time' does contain an essential truth in that the consultant's report will be determined by the way the client defines the task and supplies information. Thus before a consultant is called in management must identify the issue they want tackled and their reason for seeking assistance. This does not mean that the consultant's brief need be narrow. For example, we know a senior manager who calls in a consultant for one half-day a month to discuss how developments in management research might have implications for the company, a useful way of keeping abreast of developments which otherwise time would not permit him to follow.

Management should prepare the workforce for the arrival of a consultant by explaining exactly what task is to be undertaken. By emphasizing positive aspects of the assignment management can reduce fears of reorganization and promote staff co-operation.

Consultants can offer an enterprise extra expertise and an outsider's objective evaluation. The idea of consultancy has come into some disrepute where managers bring in consultants with an ill-defined brief or to provide a justification for unpopular policies.

Contingency Theory   Contingency theory regards the effectiveness of particular organization structures as dependent, or contingent, on the particular situation of the firm. Contingency theory is thus opposed to the universalism of *classical management* (see separate entry) and in favour of a more particularist approach where the effectiveness of any given organizational structure depends on such variables as size, technology and the nature of the environment (see *Woodward, Burns, Lawrence and Lorsch*, and the *Aston Group*). It should be added that there is not any single contingency theory; the term refers rather to the particular perspective, and is a label for a variety of theories embodying this dependency idea by linking organizational structure with something else.

Contingency Theory of Leadership   The basic idea here is that there is no one 'best way' to be a leader or exercise leadership. The effectiveness of any particular leader is contingent on the situation and the people being led (see *leadership* and *contingency theory*).

Control   The process of comparing actual performance with planned performance, and taking action in response to differences. Once a business has a plan, it is necessary to have 'control' procedures to ensure that the tasks provided for in the plan are performed properly.

There are three stages in the control process:

(a) Establish *standards* (see separate entry) specifying the planned performance of the aspect of the business under consideration.

(b) Compare actual performance achieved with the specified standard. If this is satisfactory then no further action is necessary. If this is unsatisfactory then we move to the third stage.

(c) Take corrective action. Immediate action is necessary to correct the problem and achieve the desired standard. In addition, the manager should consider whether more basic action is needed to avoid the problem arising again.

Corporate Culture The culture of a business organization is usually understood to be the sum of the common beliefs and shared understandings of its members, especially its managerial members. In this sense the corporate culture is not an absolute: it is enough that many of the members accept such beliefs much of the time, and such a state of affairs makes it reasonable to speak of the existence of a corporate culture.

The corporate culture is often held to contribute to the attainment of the formal organization's two classic needs, for:

(a) external adaptation, and

(b) internal integration.

The first, the way the company relates to its environment, may be helped by the place of the company's mission in the corporate culture, by beliefs about its objectives, about what are legitimate means of achieving them, about what is owed to society, and what it is reasonable to take from that society. Internal integration, or the holding together of the parts and members of the company, may be helped by the corporate culture serving to legitimize the company's status system, rewards structure and differential distribution of authority; the shared understandings and common meanings will facilitate communication, help to integrate new members, give a sense of identity and show that it means something to belong to this company and not some other.

The idea of corporate culture became popular in the 1980s. In part it followed naturally in Britain from a mood of national self-questioning related to economic under-performance; this led to an interest in other countries with more successful economies, and their superior achievement was often explained in cultural terms. This paved the way for an appreciation of the role of corporate culture in contributing to business success.

There has been an analogous development in the USA, in terms of that country's response to the enormous success of the Japanese on the world economic stage. In trying to understand this success Americans have attached importance to cultural factors – the motivation of Japanese employees, the *esprit de corps* of Japanese management, the patriotic underpinning of national economic success, as well as to more tangible phenomena such as quality circles and the JIT delivery system. Hence a part of the American distillation from Japan has been to urge a more Japanese ethos or culture in US companies.

The key importance of corporate culture is that a strong and functional corporate culture may make a contribution to business success. This idea is fundamental to Peters and Waterman's book *In Search of Excellence* (see *excellence*) where the key features of the successful companies are largely cultural, that is they are about values, commitments and states of mind; the success of the successful is not explained by Peters and Waterman in terms of strategy, structure or scientific decision-making.

Corporate culture is also important for explaining the success or failure of takeovers and mergers; a takeover, after all, is a corporate culture clash, and differences in the corporate culture of the firms involved may impede the successful integration of the acquired company. The same argument is relevant to the success or failure of diversification initiatives. Diversifications which fail are usually explained in terms of the company not understanding the production-market-business into which it sought to move; but it makes just as good sense to argue that, say, a successful insurance company is likely to have a corporate culture inimical to civil engineering contracting, or that automobile executives cannot culturally manage software houses.

Corporate Identity   It is estimated that in the USA companies spend some $6 bn (1987 figure) a year on revamping the way their customers, shareholders and employees see them. Often a change of name accompanies a change of image. A thorough change of identity involves changing all aspects of the company's image, from the annual report to staff uniforms.

The effects of such a change in identity are hard to quantify because often the change coincides with a change in the whole corporate strategy. Perhaps the most widely publicized flop came in the USA when United Airlines spent $7 m on an image change involving a new name, 'Allegis'; the chairman was deposed and the name change reversed! Successes are harder to quantify, but in the UK the British Airways image change is widely quoted as a success story.

Corporate Strategy   A term embracing management decisions concerning the overall direction of the organization. Decisions on strategy tend to involve:

- definition of the scope of an organization's activities
- matching the organization's activities to the *environment* (see separate entry)
- planning the activities of the organization in line with available resources
- allocating resources within the organization
- planning the long-term development of the organization
- defining the overall objectives of the organization

- assessing the needs for change in the structure of the organization to allow for changes in strategy

Broadly speaking the process of managing corporate strategy can be considered in three stages:

(a) *strategic analysis* (see separate entry), considering the challenges confronting the organization;

(b) *strategic choice* (see separate entry), considering the range of strategic options available and choosing from them;

(c) *strategic implementation* (see separate entry), implementing the plan chosen.

Corporate Venturing A corporate venture is a structured relationship between a large company, known as the 'sponsor', and a smaller company, being the 'investee'. A third party, such as a venture capital fund, may also be involved in the relationship as a provider of finance. The sponsor takes a minority interest in the investee and provides both finance and management skills, enabling the innovative talents of the smaller company to develop. Arrangements of this type are becoming increasingly common in the USA, although so far they have not developed in the UK.

Corporation Tax This is a tax imposed on the profits of companies. In the UK corporation tax is paid in two parts:

(a) Advance corporation tax is paid in proportion to the amount of any dividend payment.

(b) Mainstream corporation tax is a proportion of taxable profit for the year and is paid, after deducting any advance corporation tax that has already been paid, nine months after the balance sheet date.

There is not a great deal that a company can do to reduce the total corporation tax liability. Artificial 'tax avoidance schemes' can in practice sometimes increase the tax liability, involve substantial legal costs, and would generally not be recommended by reputable accountants. What a good accountant often can do is to help plan the company's affairs in such a way as to defer payment of taxation, so as to strengthen the *cash flow* (see separate entry) position.

Cost Managers need to know about costs for decision-making. Traditionally accounting reports focus on the costs that are actually paid for the use of a resource.

For management decision purposes the *relevant* cost is the cost that will arise as a result of the choice between two alternatives.

To give a simple example, suppose a retail business has decided to cease trading at a particular shop. The shop concerned is held on a lease with exactly one year to run at a rental of £5,000 per year. We have a choice:

(a)   We have been offered a rental of £3,000 for the remaining year of our lease by another retailer who wishes to sublet the premises from us.

(b)   The manager of the new store we have opened next door would like the use of the old premises for the one remaining year of the lease as a storage area.

In this example the managers of the business should regard the cost of allowing the use of the old shop for storage as £3,000, because this is the amount that would be lost as a result of forgoing the alternative of subletting. The fact that the actual rental paid will be £5,000 is irrelevant because this commitment has already been entered into and will not be affected by our decision.

Cost Accounting   A major aspect of *management accounting* (see separate entry), concerned with ascertaining and analysing information on *cost* (see separate entry) for management.

Countertrade   When exporting to countries with foreign exchange difficulties a business may sometimes be offered a 'countertrade' deal, whereby the customer offers payment in goods or services rather than cash. Such deals are highly complex to administer, for example, it is normally necessary to find a buyer for the bartered goods. There are also major legal complications. The UK Department of Trade has suggested that, at best, one in ten of such deals are successful. As an example, we saw a helicopter unused and apparently neglected at a Swedish airfield. We learnt that it had been acquired in a countertrade from the Soviet Union and promptly grounded under Sweden's stringent safety rules. This is definitely a proposition only to be undertaken with expert advice.

Credit   Many businesses find that they both buy and sell goods on credit terms.
The management of trade credit allowed to customers is known as 'credit control'. In establishing a credit control policy management has to settle two questions:

(a)   What risk of default is acceptable? To limit sales to the 'safest' customers may cut the level of activity excessively, while to allow credit sales to all customers may lead to unacceptably high bad debts.

(b)   How long a period of trade credit should be allowed? Sales can be increased by giving a longer period of credit, but at the cost of tying up the company's money in unproductive debtors and so increasing finance costs.

Management must also decide on how the business should conduct itself as a customer, in terms of what length of credit to take from suppliers. Most firms offer a 'discount' for prompt payment, and management must decide whether to pay early to enjoy this discount, or defer payment and so conserve the company's cash resources (see *cash flow*). Once the cash discount has been forgone, it may seem attractive to defer payment of trade creditors as long as possible and thereby enjoy the benefit of retaining cash resources in the business. Such a policy, however, can have hidden costs, including:

- The business loses goodwill with suppliers, and may suffer in terms of the quality of service received.

- If excessive trade credit is taken, suppliers may suddenly refuse to supply further goods except for immediate cash payment.

- Some suppliers, particularly small businesses, may feel unable to offer services to organizations notorious for slow payment. Many local authorities, for example, lose the opportunity of receiving tenders from low-cost small building contractors for this reason.

- Slow payment gives a business a bad name, and may actually damage the ability to *sell* goods. For example, we know a timber wholesaler who regularly receives enquiries from private customers. These enquiries are always referred to retailers who are known to pay the wholesaler promptly.

Critical Path Analysis A technique used to control complex programmes involving a series of operations. The basic steps are:

- Place all steps and their necessary sequences on a chart.

- Record the time required to complete each individual step.

- For each sequence add together the required time for each step. The longest sequence is termed the 'critical path'.

- The difference between the time for each sequence and the critical path time represents a slack period for that sequence.

Culture The term connotes different things in different disciplines. In the humanities subjects the reference is to (the best) art, music, literature and architecture of a society or period, to its study and appreciation. Anthropologists, on the other hand, use culture to denote the overall occupational or survival structure of primitive societies, as in, for instance, a hunting culture or a pastoral culture.

But it is the sociological use of the word culture which is relevant to management practice where culture is seen as the totality of a society's beliefs, values and social attitudes. Culture in this sense is not an absolute: it is no more than what most members of a society accept most of the time, with patterned exceptions, occasional dual standards and dissenting sub-groups.

Its importance for management lies in the fact that:

- Culture may constrain business organization or management practice, so that, in the West for instance, hierarchy, division of labour and formal authority are all acceptable (enshrined in the culture) but the employment of women on heavy manual work or of children on work that is dangerous is taboo.

• Culture may create opportunities. Where, for example, a culture stresses individuality it thereby favours career striving, personal achievement and thus a particular kind of remuneration package.

• Cultural considerations may affect advertising, marketing and product development. The modern view that physical toil is tedious rather than noble favours the development and sale of domestic labour saving devices, or, to give a negative example, Western culture holds that it is unthinkable to eat animals kept as pets so there will be no market for tinned dog broth or instant casseroled budgie.

The sociological notion of culture has also been adapted to explore national differences in management style and to characterize the different milieu of particular companies. See *national culture* and *corporate culture*.

Current Cost Accounting   An accounting method based on the measurement of assets and expenses by reference to their 'value' rather than historical cost. During the 1970s such an approach was proposed in a number of countries, including the USA and the UK, in response to the problems of *inflation accounting* (see separate entry). However, as the major Western economies have cut back inflation levels practical interest in this topic has declined.

Custom and Practice   A standard expression in British industrial relations, referring to the way certain things are done or arranged, and that by time-hallowed agreement, not by law or written specification. Custom and practice is usually appealed to by the representatives of workers as a justification for doing things in a certain way, keeping hold of rights or concessions they already have, or resisting (managerially) initiated change. If it is custom and practice to do it this way rather than that, then there has to be a good reason to change (or a tangible inducement).

Customer Needs   Customers are influenced by a wide range of factors in their choice of a product. Awareness of the full range of customer needs may enable managers to differentiate a basic product from that of their competitors. For example, the main services provided by the major banks to their customers are very similar. Thus a customer's choice of bank may be influenced by the range and quality of peripheral services.

Cyclical Stabilization   Sometimes an organization faces cyclical or seasonal demand for its product. Cyclical stabilization involves finding a use for resources which would otherwise be unused during the slack period. An example is the way in which many seaside resorts offer conference facilities to attract trade in the winter season.

D

Debt Covenants US term for agreed limit on the total borrowings of a business. See *borrowing powers*.

Decentralization The general case for decentralization is that it enables people at the sharp end to take decisions and engage in initiatives which seem to be justified by their immediate operating circumstances, and have room to respond to local needs.

It is possible to refine the concept of decentralization by mapping its dynamic progression:

High decentralization ↑	Investment centre
	Profit centre
	Contribution centre
Low decentralization ↓	Cost centre

At the bottom of the scale, isolating an operating unit as a cost centre is the first stage. A contribution centre is one ruled by the extent to which its revenue exceeds its direct costs, but without taking account of overheads. A profit centre is judged in terms of its profit in the sense of revenue minus total costs, but does not decide what to do with this profit, simply remitting it to its headquarters or holding company. An investment centre, on the other hand, has the right to deploy its own profits as well.

Decentralization may help motivate people by making them better informed, more responsible and giving them more control. It should also lighten the workload of managers in the operating units by removing the need for 'heavy reporting' and data provision for higher authority.

The downside is that decentralization may lead to overlapping and competition in the market place, and preclude the possibility of certain economies of scale, including the benefits of central purchasing (see *vertical integration*).

Over recent decades it is probable that decentralization has increased on a world scale, typically via the organizational form of divisionalization. Recently, however, that trend has probably been reversed where (re)centralization in response to recession and enhanced competition has been the order of the day.

There is no golden rule of centralization/decentralization; it is a case of weighing control-economies-integration against initiative-motivation-adaptation. Some studies, however, suggest that decentralization/speed of response is more appropriate in circumstances of technical or market change. It has also been noted that centralization seems to serve service industries better than manufacturing, and in particular to be associated with successful chain retailing operations.

Delegation   The passing of tasks, activities, assignments and responsibilities on to subordinates is generally held in the textbooks to be desirable and managers are ritually chastised for not doing it. That is not invariably true. To play devil's advocate for a moment, the manager who feels he cannot delegate because none of the subordinates will be able to handle the task as well as he can may well be right. In such cases the judgement will be about whether a 5% worse performance or a 15% greater risk of a foul-up is justified for the delegator in opportunity cost terms – what will he do with the time saved by delegation and how worth doing is it?

A further simplicity which arises in many discussions of delegation is the use of the Hamlet model, to delegate or not to delegate. This, typically, is not the question; the critical issue is much more likely to be what to delegate, and it matters that this should be conscious and thought out, not go by default. Most management jobs offer a number of choices, at least as regards relative emphasis, including:

- choice between technical and supervisory elements

- how much time to spend with subordinates

- whether this contact with them should be a control function or a management development one

- whether to emphasize the trouble-shooting or the systems maintenance aspect

- high or low on risk

- high or low in innovation

and so on. Now, few individuals will be equally good at all of these and, especially, few managers will lack subordinates who are not better at some of them. So assess the job, decide your options and delegate accordingly.

Delivery   Refers to the punctual delivery of manufactured output to customers, and what research findings we have suggest that it is not a British strength. There is also a study of comparative delivery performance among several Western European countries, which puts Britain bottom and Sweden and West Germany top. So it is worth enquiring as to the causes of poor delivery performance.

There are quite a lot of them, and it is usually unhelpful to go for some all-embracing explanation such as poor industrial relations. Possible causes include:

- failure by suppliers to deliver raw materials or bought-out parts, for whatever reason

- technical failure

- problems with subcontractors or co-operating companies

- disruption through strikes
- poor relations between functions/departments
- design or production engineering phase over-running
- delays at the inspection stage
- delays at the packaging/despatch stage or with transport

So what can be done to improve performance? To generalize, three things:

(a) If delivery performance is unsatisfactory, find out why, and find out systematically, not just by asking Fred what he thinks; most of the problems referred to above can be cured, masked, allowed for or ameliorated, but you have to know what problem to work on.

(b) Check the systems – is the automatic reordering system for small parts consumed in numbers working well (is there a system at all!); is the production planning/control system adequate; are inspection procedures unnecessarily cumbersome; is there a planned maintenance system; and so on.

(c) Take it seriously – part of the amazing record of the Germans in this matter is simply that they think it is important and try hard, and this disposition colours other decisions, for instance, on staffing levels and machinery purchase.

Delphi Technique   A method for using the forecasting services of a pool of experts. Each expert is asked to make a forecast in two stages:

(a) Each expert is asked to make a forecast on a specific matter, giving reasons for their prediction.

(b) These forecasts and reasons are collected, and then distributed to the other experts who are each invited to make a further individual prediction in the light of these insights.

The objective is to draw fully on the skills of each expert while, at the second stage, moving towards a consensus.

Demarcation   The line that exists between different manual jobs in the same industry. The line sometimes derives from putative skill differences, but more often simply from differences in job content; riveting, for example, is not welding, and a line demarcation is held to exist between them in the shipbuilding industry, even if welders know how to rivet and vice versa.

Demarcation has been an important issue in British industrial relations, being seen by workers and their representatives as a way of protecting jobs and keeping up trade specialism. Management responses have included:

- leaving well alone, and hoping industrial decline will be contained!

- buying out demarcations as part of productivity agreements and wage deals – the classic case is the Fawley agreement in Britain in the 1960s where Esso at their Fawley refinery outside Southampton 'bought the union rule book', i.e., bought flexibility at the price of a wage rise;

- chatting or charming workers into ignoring demarcation on a local basis when it is in management's interest – British production managers are often very good at this.

The erosion of demarcation occasionally rebounds on management. One of the authors witnessed a case where the production director abolished demarcation between welders and profile cutters; later he invited the welders to work overtime to clear a backlog of work and was told by the union rep that everyone would work overtime.

Demography The statistical study of human population. Astute businessmen pay close attention to demography in their long-term planning, both in relation to future customers and staffing.

As an example, we were congratulating the president of a large German company about his enlightened promotion of equal opportunities for women. He explained that, looking forward to the turn of the century, his company anticipated a desperate shortage of well-educated graduates, a view based on an analysis of trends in the birth rate in recent years. By creating an environment where girls at school would be encouraged to prepare for a career in industry, he hoped to ease his company's future recruitment problems.

Design A composite and variable activity embracing a creative process in the sense of imagining or conceiving new products or models, thinking what they would look like and what features they would have, and then drawing them, doing all the calculations and eventually producing prototypes and machine drawings.

De-skilling Essentially, the transfer of workers' craft, practical knowledge and elements of job control to management or to machines. This happens either as the result of increasing division of labour, or as a consequence of greater technical sophistication – mechanization, automation, computerization.

The implications for management are: be alive to the de-skilling implications of other changes, don't pretend it is not happening when it is, expect workers to resist it, and where a new technology offers a choice – e.g. CNC (computer numerically controlled) machines – do not go down the road of de-skilling if you do not have to.

Developing Countries A group of the less developed countries of the world, often referred to as the 'Third World', can be identified as tending to share certain characteristics. These include little modern industry or supporting services, low output per person and often unequal distribution of income.

Managers operating in such an environment will find that they have to

43

adapt many techniques. For example, traditional tight stock control procedures must be substantially adapted to a situation where severe commodity shortages make it essential to buy in stock when opportunities arise.

Multinational companies provide an opportunity to provide a fast start in building up such an economy, and the scale of multinational company investment in the developing countries indicates the profitable opportunities these offer. However, many developing countries suffer from political instability and in making such an investment the multinational company has to evaluate carefully the risk of expropriation of their investment. Thus management are likely to make a careful political analysis before embarking upon projects in such countries.

Development Development as in research and development (R & D) involves taking the idea for a process or product that research has shown to be possible and developing it to the point that something workable and usable is produced, if only as a 'one-off'. Most of what is loosely called R & D is in fact development, pure research being the preserve of only a small number of firms.

Diary Study Involves managers being asked to keep a record of their daily work activities for a period. The diary can serve a number of purposes:

- It identifies the way in which a manager spends time, and may be used in a time management exercise to give guidance on how time can be used more effectively.

- A management trainer may ask managers to keep such a diary in order to facilitate course design.

- The diary can be an invaluable piece of research evidence into the management process. This use was pioneered by the Swedish professor Sune *Carlson* (see separate entry).

Directive Leadership An assertive style of leadership in which the leader simply tells subordinates what they should do and how – and the emphasis is definitely on how rather than why (see *leadership*).

Discounts Reductions from an official or published price, typically for:
- buying in large numbers
- placing the order at a time convenient to the seller
- paying promptly
- being a desirable/powerful/high status customer in the eyes of the seller

From the point of view of the professional buyer making sourcing arrangements for his company, discounts are something of a commercial jungle to be hacked through. First, they are complicated, with different suppliers operating different systems on different percentages. Second, there is often a sliding scale whereby the greater the number purchased the lower the unit price. Third, there may be an element of conmanship in discount quoting in the sense that the 'basic price' that the supplier quotes and from which the discount is deducted does not really exist: so it may be best to regard the starting price as fiction and the discounted end-price as fact.

Distribution   An important aspect of any *marketing mix* (see separate entry) is the question of how the product should be distributed to the customers. This involves management in decisions about distribution channels, that is the middlemen to be involved. In an extreme case a manufacturer might sell to an agent, who sells to a wholesaler, who sells to a retailer, who sells to the consumer. Each of these roles can in turn be complicated. For example, we know a small retailer who, in order to secure discounts for bulk buying, purchases supplies in excess of her own needs and resells part of these to other retailers whose premises are at a sufficient distance not to constitute competition.

Choice of distribution channel is influenced by a number of factors, including:

- *the product*, for example, a product that needs tailoring to the customer's special needs is likely to be sold direct;

- *the enterprise*, for example, a new business with limited financial resources will tend to avoid the expense of running its own distribution channels by employing middlemen;

- *the market*, for example, if a product has a wide range of potential users then retailers are more likely to be involved.

Diversification   By diversifying the range of activities in which the enterprise is engaged managers can spread the *risk* (see separate entry) taken on each venture. Fixed costs of the enterprise are spread over an increased level of activity, and a wider range of products may help persuade dealers to specialize in a particular brand name.

At the same time, diversification places a strain on the managerial resources of the enterprise. It is often argued that diversification tends to be most successful when the enterprise has existing expertise in the production and/or marketing of the type of product concerned. See *competitive advantage*.

Divestment   Just as a company should regularly consider embarking on new ventures (see *diversification*) so it may be appropriate on occasion to dispose of part of an enterprise, this process being known as 'divestment'. The *Boston Consulting Group* (see separate entry) have suggested one approach to identifying candidates for this treatment. Where divestment is decided on, a *management buy-out* (see separate entry) is an increasingly common way of disposal.

Dog   Term used by the *Boston Consulting Group* (see separate entry) to describe a product where the company has a low market share and there is a low growth rate. It is argued that such products are best dropped.

Dow Jones Index   The most widely quoted indicator of overall price movements on the New York stock exchange. The main index is based on share price movements for thirty major industrial countries. There are also Dow Jones indices for different business sectors.

See also *Financial Times index*.

Dual Sourcing   See *purchasing*.

E

Ecology   Concern about the impact of business activity on the environment poses a growing challenge for managers. Legislation on pollution in all Western countries has become progressively tighter, posing particular problems for the small business which is unlikely to have easy access to expert advice on compliance. In the USA research has shown the costs of coping with ecological requirements to be a major source of concern for the presidents of small companies. The prudent manager will ensure that any planned business activity not only complies with existing legal requirements but can also be adapted to meet any likely future restrictions.

Economic Order Quantity   An important aspect of *stock control* (see separate entry) is to determine the quantity of an item that should be ordered when a new batch is required. This is known as the economic order quantity, and is influenced by price (which may vary with batch size), storage costs, interest charges on money borrowed to finance stock, transport costs, deterioration risks, handling costs and administrative costs.

Economies of Scale   As a business expands economies of scale can be achieved. This is for two reasons:

(a)   fixed costs can be spread over a greater number of units of production, for example, the costs of developing a new product will not increase in proportion to the number produced;

(b)   variable costs per unit may also be reduced with increased production, for example, the unit cost of raw materials may be reduced by bulk buying.

On the other hand, as a business expands new management styles have to be developed. Moreover, a larger business may have difficulty in responding in a flexible way to changes in the environment. A large business may try to continue to enjoy the benefits of economies of scale while at the same time recreating the atmosphere of a new enterprising business in areas of innovation. Ways of doing this include allowing a development team a high degree of autonomy (for example, see *skunk works*) or allowing a development team to take a major financial stake in the project (for example, see *sponsored spin-out*).

Economy   A measure of the quantity of resources consumed in pursuing an objective. See *value for money*.

Edwardes, Michael   South African born British business manager, who made a long-term, successful career at Chloride but is best known for his few years at British Leyland. Confident and energetic with a high profile style, he was an uncompromising challenger of shop steward power at BL. These and other adventures are described in his autobiographical work *Back from the Brink* (Collins, London, 1983); for a comparison of British and American style and content it should be read side by side with Lee Iacocca's autobiography (see *Iacocca*).

Effectiveness   A measure of the extent to which an objective has been achieved. See *value for money*.

Efficiency   A measure of the level of output achieved compared to the level of input consumed. See *value for money* and *productivity*.

Electronic Fund Transfer Point Of Sale (EFTPOS)   The payment system in retail outlets ranging from supermarkets to petrol stations whereby the purchaser has a debit card 'wiped' at the checkout and his bank account is instantly debited for the amount of the purchase (insteady of paying by cash, cheque or credit card). The advantages include:

- shorter queues at checkouts
- big step towards the convenience of cashlessness
- improved cash flow for retailers
- built-in accounting, recording and stock control facilities
- profits for those who make the kit

The downside for customers is that they need enough money in their accounts to cover purchases at the time they are made!

Employers' Federations   An industry may have a federation of employers formed to manage such matters as collective bargaining with members or to deal with trade matters. The particular needs of the industry tend to influence the role of the federation. For example, in the UK building trade workers often are employed by a number of different firms in a year, so the employers' federation co-ordinates a holiday pay scheme.

Companies sometimes find that the rules of such a federation are a hindrance. For example, we know a businessman who some years ago decided to resign from his trade federation in order to avoid a rule against price cutting (such a rule would in most industries probably now be unlawful). As a result he expanded his trade by 400%.

Engineers In all industrialized countries, there is an empirical overlap between engineers and managers. Even in Britain, with its popular reputation for engaging arts graduate generalists, among those managers who are graduates more have degrees in engineering than in anything else. At the strong end of the spectrum are countries, such as West Germany, where qualified engineers dominate all the technical functions including production, overspill into the commercial functions, and are heavily represented in top management if only by sheer weight of numbers.

The predominance of engineers in management is associated with a high standing for the technical functions and an emphasis on design, production methods and quality. There may be a corresponding neglect of marketing (as opposed to sales), management systems and corporate policy – such criticisms were levelled against, for instance, West Germany in the 1970s.

Enterprise Zones In the UK the government has, during the 1980s, designated an increasing number of run-down inner city areas as 'enterprise zones'. Businesses setting up inside such zones enjoy various fiscal incentives and reduced controls on planning. Two problems arise:

(a) It is hard to tell whether such a policy creates additional jobs or merely attracts jobs from other areas.

(b) To a large extent such incentives tend to result in increased land prices or rentals, so that the benefits go to landowners rather than to business.

Entertainment Business entertaining, despite the discouragement of the taxman and the disapproval of the puritanical, is a major activity in most Western economies. For example, for 1987 UK corporate entertaining is estimated to cost some £500 m.

Some companies, looking beyond the traditional hospitality tents at sporting functions and block bookings for cultural events, sponsor an entire event thereby combining publicity with the chance to exclude competitors. Sports and cultural promoters looking for sponsorship could benefit from growth in this area.

Entrepreneurs People with the ability to create a working enterprise where none existed before. The entrepreneur produces the combination of ideas, skills, money, equipment and markets which form a successful business. Several studies have shown that most entrepreneurs are motivated by a search for security, which they feel can only be achieved by controlling their own work environment. This leads to considerable problems when the business expands, because the entrepreneur is reluctant to let control of the activities of the business pass to a management team. Thus the manager invited to join a company still dominated by the founding entrepreneur should view the opportunity with some caution.

Entry Barrier Anything that stops a company entering a new market, typically

- the cost of setting up new manufacture

- existing products protected by patent

- dominance of others already serving in the particular market, especially through monopolization of distribution channels

Entry barriers have on the whole declined in the 1980s, due to more flexible technologies and a decline in smoke-stack, heavy investment industries. So, everyone has a greater opportunity to invade everyone else's markets. The message is: make sure you do it to them before they do it to you.

Environment Managers of any enterprise need to be aware of the host of ways in which changes in various aspects of the environment can affect business. To take a few examples:

- *The economic environment.* For example, we know a steel manufacturer in a small country whose dependence on imports and exports makes prediction of currency movements the most important element in determining profit.

- *Customer tastes.* In the UK the major breweries found in the early 1970s that they had to respond to a major consumer movement in support of traditional beers.

- *Competitors.* We know a major UK manufacturer who stayed out of a major section of their traditional market for several years because their major competitor priced their product at an uneconomic level. They resumed production when the competitor went bankrupt!

An analysis of changes and potential changes in the environment is essential in the formulation of *corporate strategy* (see separate entry).

Ergonomics 'Human engineering' is the term most commonly used in the USA for ergonomics. It involves the study of the relationship between man and his working environment. The objective is to produce machines and equipment which can be used with the minimum of physical and mental strain, applying a knowledge of anatomy, physiology and psychology.

Management can improve productivity and reduce absenteeism by applying ergonomic principles to both the acquisition and the layout of equipment used in offices and factories. As an example, laboratory experiments have shown that background noise affects different kinds of work in different ways, having an adverse effect on jobs requiring concentration and sometimes even a beneficial effect on the performance of simple repetitive tasks. Thus if a manager has to choose between machines for use in a task, the ergonomist would offer advice on the importance of the noise level which would be influenced by an evaluation of the type of work to be done near the machine.

An awareness of ergonomic principles is also of increasing importance in product design.

Ethics Managers may from time to time be faced with a decision that poses an ethical problem. Awareness that a practice is ethically undesirable may come from social values, often expressed in legislation, from a professional code of conduct, from the company's own code of conduct or from the manager's own moral values.

It is in the nature of such problems that the manager will face potential penalties whichever approach he chooses. We know, for example, a manager who, on behalf of his employer, made false statements to secure an increased business commission; his conduct was discovered and resulted in a criminal prosecution. Equally, there is a UK case in which an accountant disclosed his employer's attempt to overcharge on a government contract, which resulted in the man's dismissal and a long period of unemployment.

If this is not a comforting statement of the position, a recent survey was more cheering. It found that 53% of managers interviewed had faced a conflict between ethical values and their employers' requirements. Of those 67% stood by their ethical position, and of those 70% suffered no penalty. The position of such a manager is less lonely than it might appear.

European Community Managers operating in or trading with any of the European Community (EC) member states should be aware of the potential impact of the Community on their business.

In principle the Community should make life easier for the manager, as the harmonization of regulations and the dismantling of trade barriers bring nearer the objective of Europe as a single market. The larger companies are increasingly operating as European rather than national entities, and managers in such companies may well find themselves in jobs in several countries during their careers.

Managers need to have an eye on the way in which harmonization is likely to affect their own domestic markets.

European Monetary System (EMS) An arrangement within the EC subscribed to by most members, though not currently (mid 1988) by the UK, to restrict fluctuations between their currencies. Members of the EMS collaborate to intervene in the markets to restrict fluctuations, and also try to apply compatible domestic economic policies. In practice during the history of the

EMS a number of currency realignments have proved necessary. There is a major debate as to whether the UK should join the EMS. Advocates argue that business would benefit from reduction in uncertainty about currency movements. Opponents dislike the idea of accepting an external discipline on domestic economic policy, and also argue that the UK as a major oil producer faces a different currency environment to other EMS members.

Excellence   Cult term of the 1980s referring to qualities of corporate performance, assessed in financial terms and attributed to a 'quality' ethic. The concept began with the publication in 1982 of the widely acclaimed book *In Search of Excellence* by Thomas Peters and Robert Waterman (Harper & Row, New York). The authors established six financial performance criteria, applied them to American corporations over a twenty year period, and thus selected the 'excellent' companies, the high performers. The book then sought to characterize these excellent companies, to say what was different and interesting about them. In short they were said to be distinguished by:

- a bias for action
- being close to the customer
- autonomy and entrepreneurship
- productivity through people
- being hands-on, value driven
- doing what they know best
- having a simple form, with lean staff
- having simultaneous loose–tight properties, i.e., controlling one or two key things closely while allowing considerable freedom in everything else

In Search of Excellence inspired a British response in the form of a book by Walter Goldsmith and David Clutterbuck *The Winning Streak* (Weidenfeld & Nicolson, London), published in 1984, though this English study was more impressionistic than the American original. Both sets of authors published follow-up works as the decade proceeded, and conferences on the theme of excellence abounded.

A by-product was the 'Who's Excellent Now?' reaction, a sub-movement taking its title from a *Harvard Business Review* article drawing attention to the fact that some of the Peters and Waterman excellent companies were then in financial difficulties. This critical counter-movement was fuelled by a methodological critique of the 'excellence studies' and by the difficulty of establishing whether features of excellent companies were causes or consequences of their excellence.

Executive Director   Member of a board of directors who is a full-time salaried manager in the company concerned. Executive directors are most

51

often the heads of particular functions within the firm – sales, personnel, R & D and so on. See also *non-executive director*.

Exit Barrier   Any obstacle to a company's leaving a market, even if there is a good reason to quit, usually declining profitability, whether deriving from enhanced competition or product life cycle.

Exit barriers are most often depicted in terms of investment in productive equipment, but less obvious is the effect of market exit on reputation and customers. The latter may well react negatively to what they see as a failure of the seller to offer the full product range or the withdrawal of an ancillary product or service. After all, most of us would be annoyed if supermarkets stopped selling loaves of bread, though from the seller's standpoint bread is a poor proposition – low mark-up, short shelf-life and takes up to much space in relation to its value.

Two practical messages:

(a)   Before withdrawing, ask what the effect will be on customers as well as on the balance sheet.

(b)   Think twice about entering a market where the exit barriers are high (consider Israel's flirtation with shipbuilding).

Expectancy Theory   A development in thinking about motivation that calls into question the links in the chain:

individual – effort – performance – rewards

The authorized version is that individuals (employees, managers) who seek rewards exert effort to achieve effective performance which results in obtaining the desired reward. Expectancy theory, however, suggests that the individual's willingness to engage in the effort is actually conditional on three expectations:

(a)   his or her heightened effort will actually lead to the desired performance;

(b)   this effective performance will qualify for reward;

(c)   attractive rewards are available.

Expectancy theory has a practical import in that it soberly demonstrates the environmental limits to what may be achieved in output or performance terms by able supervision or effective leadership. In circumstances, for example, of stagnation, contraction or diminishing organizational resources, it may be very difficult for superiors to motivate, whatever their personal skills. And in the reverse situation, rather less in the way of skills may be required to unleash reward-seeking effort.

Export Credit Guarantee   In the UK the Export Credit Guarantee Department (ECGD) of the Department of Trade supports export activity in a number of ways, including:

- ECGD will, by agreement, provide insurance up to 85–90% of the value of credit sales to foreign buyers.

- ECGD will also offer guarantees to commercial banks to finance large-scale projects undertaken for foreign customers.

Fees for these services are set at a level designed to cover related costs.

Export Sales The salesman operating abroad faces additional problems to those found in the domestic market. He is remote from the normal head office back-up facilities, and may be faced with customer requirements substantially different from those found at home. Thus the export salesman needs a high degree of technical knowledge. Research has shown that companies find that they need to give salesmen operating abroad a greater range of discretion than at home, so that customer requirements can be met properly.

Some companies employ local representatives in foreign countries. This gets round the language problem and may also help gain access to local contacts. However, a new communication problem can then arise between the company and the salesman, who may not relate easily to the company's culture. In some foreign countries local wage rates may be difficult to match. In a country where export sales are not high, it may be difficult to offer local sales staff a satisfactory career structure.

Broadly speaking, the more technically complex a product the more likely it is that a company will use home-based staff for foreign sales.

F

Fast-moving Consumer Goods (FMCG) As opposed to capital goods, or consumer goods such as cars or refrigerators which an individual purchases only intermittently. FMCGs are typically branded products such as cigarettes, packaged foods and patented medicines, which are bought often by lots of people.

The FMCG operation is distinctive in that:

- the distribution system is especially important;

- it offers the maximum leverage for promotional advertising (as opposed to personal selling).

Much of the marketing literature is implicitly oriented to FMCGs.

Fayol, Henri French mining engineer and founder of the classical management movement. Fayol trained as a mining engineer, rapidly became the manager of a coal mine and eventual managing director of a mining group. This group at the time of his accession was nearly bankrupt; Fayol turned it round, increased its size, and ran it for almost 30 years. His reflections and experiences led him to try to analyse the nature of the management task and formulate precepts for its effective execution. The definitive second edition of his book *L'administration générale et industrielle*, published in 1916, is usually seen as marking the start of the classical management movement, with its emphasis on right practice and general principles of administration. See *classical management*.

Federated Marketing   Small companies tend not to venture into export markets because of the costs of marketing. One solution is a 'federated marketing' approach whereby a group of companies with complementary, but not competing, products set up an independent operation to handle marketing for them in a foreign country. One of the partners in the scheme should be a management firm whose role is to balance the interests of the other partners, being remunerated by some form of management fee. Thus the management firm provides both professional expertise and a mediating role. This system is designed to get round the problems of a simple marketing consortium where each company may be suspicious of other members getting an unfair share of promotional effort.

Feedback   Providing employees, especially at junior–middle management level, with some, preferably objective, judgement on their job performance:

- to raise their awareness;

- to keep open boss–subordinate communication channels;

- in the expectation that this feedback will motivate recipients, giving recognition for a good job done, and indicating areas of possible improvement.

See also *appraisal*.

Finance   Finance as a management function might be defined as the management of money to promote the objectives of the business. Thus finance embraces the issue of how the firm should invest the financial resources – choosing between business projects – and also the issue of how money should be raised. Finance also embraces day-to-day money management, a particularly complex task when international transactions are involved.

Financial Accounting   A broad term embracing the preparation and presentation of the regular (normally annual) accounts of the business. The accounts normally consist of a *balance sheet* (see separate entry) and a profit and loss account (see *profit*) together with supporting notes. In the case of a limited company these accounts must be filed with the Registrar of Companies and can be inspected on payment of a modest fee (currently £1).

Managers, who have access to the internal accounting records of the business, are unlikely to make direct use of their own financial accounts for decision-making. For that purpose they will need more detailed and timely information. However, managers should be interested in the financial accounts of their business for a number of reasons, including:

- The picture given by the financial accounts will affect the way that outsiders, such as the bank, view the business.

- Where the accounts are subject to an audit (see *auditing*) then the audit process may throw up useful information on the accounting system.

- The figures in the accounts may influence the economic position of the business because they form the basis of some financial commitment, e.g., in the computation of *borrowing powers* (see separate entry).

- Information collected specially to meet financial accounting requirements might be useful for management purposes.

Financial Times (FT) Index   The most widely quoted indicator of overall price movements on the London stock exchange. The main FT index is the 'industrial ordinary', which is based on share price movements for thirty major industrial companies. There are also FT indices for different business sectors.

See also *Dow Jones Index*.

Focused Factory   The expression was coined by American management writer Wickham Skinner, a specialist in *manufacturing policy* (see separate entry). His basic idea is that production cannot be organized/laid out in such a way as to serve all ends, that there has to be some trade-off between such variables as capacity and flexibility, cost and quality. To achieve this trade-off a manufacturing policy must be consciously developed, one that identifies the priorities, capacity or flexibility or whatever, and then devises what Skinner calls an equipment process technology to suit the attainment of those priorities. A focused factory is one in which in Skinner's sense the equipment process technology is congruent with manufacturing policy objectives.

Forecasting   Analysis of the *environment* (see separate entry) is an essential part of the formulation of *corporate strategy* (see separate entry). Long-term decisions involve an assessment of the future environment, leading to a need for forecasts. Thus management need to identify the critical aspects of the environment, develop techniques to forecast changes in these areas, and feed the conclusions into the planning process.

Forecasting techniques depend on the subject matter considered. For example, future population changes can be predicted on the basis of recent birth rates (see *demography* for a practical example). Some economic indicators are identifiable by market movements. For example, if the 'forward' price of a foreign currency is lower than the current exchange rate then clearly the markets expect that currency to weaken. For some broader aspects of the environment outside experts might be consulted.

Foundation for Management Education (FME)   Founded in the UK in 1960, the FME promotes management education at university level. The FME works to enhance the quality of management teachers, to encourage the development of research, to consider innovative developments in management education, and to develop better teaching techniques. To advance these aims FME has raised substantial funds from industry, and has also acted as a catalyst in bringing business and universities together.

Four Ps   E. Jerome McCarthy, an American, has put forward the idea that the marketing activities of a business can be considered under four headings. These can be remembered by a simple mnemonic, the 'four Ps', being 'product', 'price', 'place' and 'promotion'.

'Product' embraces everything concerned with the features of the actual goods or services offered, including not only the quality, design and durability of the product itself, but also accompanying features such as service back-up and warranty.

'Price' incorporates not only the unit price of the product but also other financial elements such as trade-in prices and credit terms. Price considerations also include the price of other elements to be sold relating to the product, such as accessories and service.

'Place' concerns the distribution arrangements whereby goods are made available to customers. Decisions on this aspect cover both the physical arrangements, such as locations of outlets and means of transport, and institutional arrangements, such as choosing whether to use wholesalers and retailers.

'Promotion' embraces personal selling as well as advertising and other forms of selling promotion, packaging and display.

The company's combination of these activities makes up the *marketing mix* (see separate entry).

Franchising   A common form of *joint venture* (see separate entry) where an enterprise with a distinctive product (the franchiser) agrees to allow another enterprise (the franchisee) to distribute the product in a specified area. One of the best known examples is the Coca Cola company whose franchise holders manufacture, bottle and distribute the product. Franchising allows an enterprise to expand distribution of the product rapidly with limited financial and managerial resources.

Fringe Benefits   Anything having a material value actually or potentially enjoyed by employees apart from the traditional wage or salary. The range is enormous, from free uniforms to private school fees, from the right to buy 'seconds' at a discount to stock options.

There is a lot of variation in fringe benefits from country to country. Managerial fringe benefits tend to be high in countries where managers are poorly paid (UK) unless the country is socialist (Sweden). Worker benefits tend to be high where welfare state provision is low (USA), unless the trade union movement provides the benefits (Israel), and so on. This is a practical issue for multinationals and their personnel policies.

There is also an element of fashion in fringe benefits. The 1980s have favoured stock options and performance linked remuneration for executives, much to the benefit of consultancies who 'installed' the schemes.

G

Gearing Most commonly used to refer to the effect of financial structure on a business. Broadly speaking, a business can obtain finance from two sources:

(a) The proprietors (shareholders in a company) can invest their own money in the business, and plough back part of the profits they earn. In return they will receive part of any profits that are earned, being paid out as dividends in the case of a company.

(b) The business can also borrow money. Lenders will normally have to be paid an agreed fixed rate of interest.

The higher the proportion of borrowing in relation to equity, the higher 'geared' the business is said to be.

Gearing has two major effects:

(a) The higher the gearing, the higher the risk that the business will have difficulty in repaying loans.

(b) High gearing means that there is a high fixed interest payment that has to be made each year, irrespective of the level of profit. Because this claim is fixed, any fluctuation in trading profit is magnified in its impact on the proprietors, who are only entitled to the residue of profit after all other claims have been met.

Gilbreth, Frank Bunker Bricklayer, building contractor and founder member of the American scientific management movement, Gilbreth developed the application of motion study in the building industry, together with incentive payment schemes. He was also a happily married, exuberant family man with twelve children, celebrated in a popular book by his son Frank and daughter Ernestine (*Cheaper by the Dozen*, William Heinemann, London, 1949). After his premature death in middle age his work as a consultant was continued by his wife Lilian. See *scientific management*.

Goal Congruence Any organization is made up of people who have individual personal goals. The art of management is to achieve 'goal con-

57

gruence' whereby the individuals within an organization are motivated to working towards the goals of the organization by matching achievement with promotion of their own goals.

As an example, we know an organization where at a certain level of management managers only receive a company car if they have to cover a specified minimum business mileage each year. A buyer therefore made a point of creating situations where he had to drive to suppliers to collect urgently required goods for the business, so as to demonstrate his need for a company car. Thus the business had created a situation where to achieve his own goal (a company car) the employee behaved in an economically inefficient way — an example of failure to achieve goal congruence.

Goal Displacement In organization theory term used to denote a situation where an avowed goal or objective is quietly moved sideways and a different objective comes to the fore, without anyone planning or intending this. Often there are incremental changes in a company's business which in the middle term amount to goal displacement. An entrepreneur establishes a small factory to make furniture, for example, and later adds a showroom to sell his product direct to the general public. This increases revenue, so he enlarges the showroom, and starts to sell furniture made by other manufacturers as well. Five years later 95% of his revenue comes from factoring – the business has become a retail operation with a factory welded on.

Goal displacement may also occur at a more modest level within the organization. Control systems, for instance, often provoke subverting behaviour, so that the goal for the employee is 'beating the system' not achieving the system objective. There is a fascinating American study of a state employment agency where a new supervisor instituted a set of published performance controls for interviewers, including number of interviews held, together with job referrals and placements as a proportion of interviews (Peter Blau, *The Dynamics of Bureaucracy*, University of Chicago Press, 1955). The interviewers responded with behaviours including concealing job vacancies from each other, downgrading the counselling side of their work as it did not lead directly to placements, giving priority to unemployed negroes who were not so choosy about what jobs they would take, and even counting as successful placements employees seasonally laid off and then re-employed – all to beat the numbers.

Goodwill A business will have a value as a whole that is different to the total value of the tangible assets it owns. This difference may be positive or negative. It arises because of a whole host of factors, such as established connections with customers or suppliers, reputation and the accumulated skills of the workforce. The difference is known as goodwill, and should normally be positive since we would expect the owners of a business with negative goodwill to increase the value of what they own by selling the business assets and realizing the proceeds.

Greenmail   This expression came into use in 1986, a year which saw 14,000 takeovers and 3,500 mergers in the USA. Greenmailing is where a raider (he who would take over a company) buys shares in a company as a preliminary to mounting a takeover attack, but then allows the target company to buy them back – at a higher price – in order to avert the takeover bid.

Groupthink   A concept developed to analyse several dubious (group) decisions in post-war American foreign policy in Korea (advancing to the Yalu river), Cuba (Bay of Pigs) and Vietnam (escalation). The essence of groupthink is that group members tend to rationalize any challenge to the assumptions they have made, and apply pressure to deviants to bring them into line. This makes dissenters unsure of their ground and reluctant to voice 'minority opinions'. The group takes over.

The problem with groupthink is knowing when it is happening, and as there are not any rules for identifying it it is best to be on guard all the time. Remember the board of directors is a group!

See also *risky-shift*.

H

Harvard Method   Teaching based on intensive use of case study material derived from real-life cases. See *case study*.

Head Office   The classic functions of head office are corporate policy and goal setting, macro resource allocation and control, all supported by a persistent information gathering exercise.

The esteem in which the head office mission is held tends to fluctuate. In the climate of the late 1980s, with its increased regard for the results-oriented line manager, head office is somewhat in eclipse, the victim of the Peters and Waterman dictum of 'strong line, lean staff' (see *excellence*).

The head office mission is indeed difficult to fulfil with the need to guide without stifling, to control without crushing. This is suffused by the further paradox that only head office produces strategy, and only it is structurally removed from a first-hand acquaintance with operations.

Hersey, P. and Blanchard, K.H.   Researchers who have contributed to the view that *leadership* (see separate entry) is contingent, that is to say, one cannot talk about good or bad leadership in general terms, only about leadership suitable in particular situations (contingencies). They are the authors of *Management Organizational Behaviour* (Prentice-Hall, Englewood Cliffs, NJ, 1977).

For Hersey and Blanchard the critical contingency is the maturity of employees, and they cross this idea with the task-centred and people-centred variables of *Blake's grid* (see separate entry). The result is a potential trajectory of styles as the maturity of employees increases.

For 'immature' employees who tend not be be committed to the task in hand, and are unwilling to take responsibility and set their own goals, the *telling* style of leadership is appropriate, that is, supervisors who are high on task and low on people concern tell them to get on with it. As employee maturity increases in terms of motivation, commitment and competence, the supervisor may move to a *selling* style in which employees are still assigned tasks and supervised, but further benefit can also be gained from working at the human relationship.

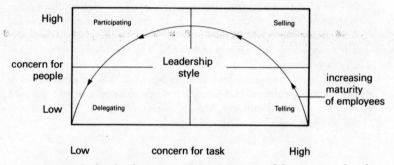

Hersey and Blanchard see it as an important part of the supervisor's task to increase employee maturity over time so that supervisory style may eventually change. The selling style they see as likely to remain the most effective approach. But if employee maturity is greater then employees will not need so much task supervision, and they can be involved in goal-setting and decision-making using a *participative* style. The most committed and capable employees will need very little relationship with their supervisor either of a task or social nature, and in such a situation the *delegative* style is appropriate.

Herzberg, Frederick   See *hygiene factors and motivators*.

Hierarchy   Refers to the system of graded ranks in an organization, constituting a line of command and a formal upward–downward communication channel.

The principal function of hierarchy is co-ordination. Disparate but complementary activities conducted in sections A and B, for example, are co-ordinated at the next (hierarchical) level up to whom the heads of A and B report. And in so far as the ranks in the hierarchy embody different amounts of prestige in ascending order, then further ends may be served (see *status*).

Having said this it is clear that there is nothing absolute about hierarchy in that hierarchies differ in length and importance. As long ago as the 1950s, for instance, research showed that companies in process industries typically have longer hierarchies than those in unit and small batch production, with mass production companies in between. Or again, comparative research in the 1970s shows that, holding size and branch of industry constant, companies in France have much longer hierarchies than those in West Germany, with British companies falling in between. Finally there are also some organizations whose hierarchies do not function as a chain of command or serve the ends of co-ordination – often this is true of educational organizations – so that the hierarchy is best understood as formalized status (see *status*).

Horizontal Integration The process whereby companies may expand 'sideways' by acquisition or merger with comparable companies making the same approximate range of goods or offering similar services. In the USA, for example, General Motors grew in the 1920s by acquiring other automobile manufacturers; in Britain the same process occurred with government support in the 1960s, producing British Leyland. Nor is the strategy restricted to manufacturing organizations. In Britain again the Westminster Bank merged with the District Bank and National Provincial Bank in 1970, thus producing the largest domestic chain.

The advantages to be reaped from horizontal integration are

- scale economies in the organization of manufacture;

- market dominance, or at least a higher degree of it;

- greater bargaining power with labour unions, suppliers and even governments deriving simply from enhanced size.

The corresponding threats are the corporate somnolence that sometimes marks large and secure companies, together with possible government intervention against an organization seen to achieve monopoly status through horizontal integration.

Human Relations A movement in motivation theory and factory supervision, starting with the Hawthorne experiments in the USA in the 1930s which showed the importance to employees of group membership and social cohesion, and popularized by Elton Mayo. The basic tenets of the human relations school are:

- financial incentives are not as important as people used to think;

- people have social affiliative needs which they will satisfy in work-groups at their place of employment;

- this group cohesion may enhance both morale and output;

- people will respond to special treatment (the Hawthorne effect);

- people respond to the right treatment in the sense of the social skills and people-centred approach of supervisors;

- the workplace as a community may be enhanced by improved conditions and amenities, indeed by making it more than just a place of work (sports clubs, hobby groups, open days for the family, and so on).

Some of these precepts may be used manipulatively, and a subsequent generation exposed the unreality of 'the factory as happy family' side by side with the differences in real interest between managers and workers and actual trade union *v.* employer conflict. Nonetheless, the human relations movement has left a permanent legacy. It has changed supervisory styles, led to an improvement in amenities and facilities at work, and been a dimension in the growth of a professional personnel management function in industry. See also *neo-human relations*.

Hygiene Factors and Motivators Frederick Herzberg produced what is known as the two-factor theory of motivation. The essence of it is that the factors which, when positive, lead to satisfaction do not, when negative, lead to dissatisfaction. Conversely, the factors which, when negative, lead to dissatisfaction do not, when positive, lead to satisfaction. Praise, for example, may be a powerful motivator, but the absence of praise may not be demotivating; or again, bad pay demotivates, but good pay is simply taken for granted.

So, according to Herzberg, we have 'motivators' whose presence heightens job satisfaction:

Achievement
Recognition
The work itself $\Big\}$ Motivators
Responsibility
Advancement

Higher performance

And we have another set of factors, 'hygiene factors', whose absence leads to dissatisfaction or dissatisfaction ensues when something is wrong in one of these areas:

Hygiene factors $\Big\{$
Company pay policy
Supervision
Salary
Interpersonal relations
Working conditions

Job dissatisfaction

Herzberg's ideas derived mainly from interviews with engineers and accountants, and are seen as having primary relevance to managers and professionals. There is later research evidence (see *Blake's grid*) to suggest that successful managers in personal career terms are those who focus on the motivators.

I

Iacocca, Lee   One time chief executive of Ford (father of the Mustang) until he lost favour with the head of the Ford dynasty. He then became head of Chrysler, achieving a spectacular turn-round of Chrysler fortunes and repaying a federal loan ahead of schedule. He produced a gutsy and readable autobiography in 1984.

Import Business   Although the term covers a variety of operations, there are a few precepts which hold a lot of the time. First, make sure the market is worth being in (e.g., as regards demand, stability and margins). Then try to get a larger share of it by achieving sole agent status with regard to overseas suppliers. Suppliers must be chosen on the basis of product quality and service, not just price – the price matters to you, but the quality and service have to be good enough for your customers, and the importer is more dependent than the manufacturer. Suppliers in turn may be kept happy by agent performance (your ability to sell their products in your market) and by prompt payment: where suppliers offer a discount it may actually pay to borrow money to settle early. Looking at the other end of the operation, it is usually an advantage to offer customers the *complete* range of products and accessories – it will stop them having to go somewhere else. And some import businesses open up the possibility of an advisory-consultancy service to customers in support of the goods supplied. If it is relevant, do it; it is a pure service, you can charge what you like for it at the specialist knowledge end of the spectrum, and its provision will mark you off from other firms that just handle the goods.

Industrial Action   Paradoxically, this phrase in English signifies industrial inaction in the sense of a restriction of output resulting from strike action, work-to-rule, or go-slow.

Industrial Democracy   System of worker representation in companies required by law in a number of European countries, including Benelux, Scandinavia, West Germany, and some east European states of which the system in Yugoslavia is probably the best known in the West. Usually it takes the form of elected works councils with defined rights and powers, sometimes supplemented by worker directors (see *works council, works committee* and *worker directors*). Certainly the evidence from Western Europe suggests that fears that industrial democracy will lead to the emasculation of management are much exaggerated.

The middle-term results might be generalized as:

- some loss of management initiative;

- but gain in industrial peace and predictableness;

- decision-making slower (need for consultation);

- implementation faster (problems already taken out by consultative process).

Industrial Relations   Relations between employer and employees. In practice, the phrase tends to denote problems, especially days lost through strikes. This industrial relations phenomenon receded somewhat in the 1980s given the recession at the start of the decade and the persistently high levels of un-employment. It will not, however, have gone for ever, and in so far as industrial relations friction is a challenge to companies, there are some considerations to keep in mind:

- Many strikes are predictable, loosely on the basis of past experience and circumstance (but see *wildcat strikes*).

- Strikes are only the tip of the iceberg below which there is a miscellany of time-consuming grievances about conditions and supervision, overtime, subcontracting, safety and recognition issues – and more besides; there is some advantage to be gained by trying to reduce this volume
    - (a) by supervisor training;
    - (b) by experiments in worker representation.

- Put your house in order; management weakness will be exploited, so, for example, remove anomalies of pay and conditions, let Personnel control precedent and regulation, don't violate safety regulations, and care for employee health.

- Expect some industrial relations friction; it is advisable to allow for it in manufacturing lead times and operational planning.

Industrial Society, The   Originally set up in the UK as the Industrial Welfare Society in 1919, the Industrial Society has as its prime aim to promote the best uses of human resources in industry. The Society works to improve leadership qualities, to promote harmony between management and unions, to improve employment conditions, to develop better communications in industry, and to develop young employees. To achieve these ends the Society offers a range of courses and publications, as well as advice on specific industrial problems.

Inertia Selling   The practice of selling people things they have not asked for and deeming them to have been 'bought' if not returned in a given period ('buyers' are then invited to pay). Morally and increasingly legislatively frowned on, the practice has a parallel in industrial selling which does not cause any raised eyebrows. This is the time-honoured practice by suppliers of sending quite legitimate buyers more than they ordered – and then invoicing them. It cannot be done with Boeing 747s (someone would notice) but works well with low-cost components supplied in large numbers. As a tactic for increasing sales revenue without incurring corresponding promotional costs it does achieve a certain success.

Inflation A major political issue in all the Western economies is the control of inflation. In public discussion inflation is generally regarded as the movement in prices experienced by consumers, measured in the UK by the Retail Price Index. However, in practice all prices do not move in unison, so that the costs of goods purchased by a business may move at a different rate, or even in a different direction, to the general level of inflation. It is important that managers make their plans based on the price level changes experienced by their own business rather than the general level of inflation.

Inflation Accounting We all know that with inflation the value of money changes every year. Traditionally accountants use money as the unit of measurement. This is a bit like an engineer trying to work with an elastic tape measure! Two possible remedies have been discussed by accountants:

(a) *Current purchasing power* (CPP) uses a general price index to adjust all the figures in the accounts to the value of money at the balance sheet date. The problem is that the individual business may have a very different experience of price changes to the general price level.

(b) *Current cost accounting* (CCA) tries to measure items in the accounts at their current value (normally replacement cost) rather than historical cost. This system is complex and expensive to apply in practice, and there are a number of technical problems in its application on which accountants are unable to agree.

During the 1970s the accounting profession both in the USA and the UK put forward a number of proposals for inflation accounting. With the reduction of inflation in the 1980s this topic has been effectively abandoned by working accountants.

In the absence of an agreed inflation accounting system working managers should be aware of the following deficiencies in traditional historic cost accounts during an inflationary period:

- Successive years' accounts are not truly comparable, because the money amounts they express represent different values. For example, a company with increased sales measured in money might in fact be selling a lower volume of goods.

- Depreciation of assets measured at the cost when they were purchased fails to reflect the amount that needs to be put aside for when the assets are replaced.

- Profit on sales measured by deducting the historic cost of stock from sales fails to reflect the extra cost of replacing stock consumed at a higher price.

- If we lend money in times of inflation we lose out because the money we get paid back in is 'worth' less. Conversely we gain from borrowing. Historical cost accounts fail to report these gains or losses.

Information Inductance   When a manager is required to supply information on his performance he can reasonably expect to be judged on that information. Thus we have an 'information inductance' effect, whereby the information managers are required to provide leads them to run their organization in a way that maximizes their apparent achievement.

We can illustrate this effect with a story which is widely quoted, though we cannot vouch for its authenticity. It is said that after the Russian Revolution nail factories in the Soviet Union were told to report to central government on the number of nails produced. As a result all Russian nail factories concentrated on the production of tin tacks, being the most economic type of nail to produce. Alerted to this difficulty by the absence of any other type of nail from production, the government revised their requirement to a report on the weight of nails produced. A glut of the largest type of nail, requiring minimum labour content for the weight produced, duly followed!

Information Revolution   The capacities of modern computer systems are expanding rapidly, costs of computer equipment are coming down rapidly, and various organizations are making available large databases. Thus the manager is given the opportunity both to collect detailed data from within the firm and to have access to a vast amount of data about the environment. The 'information revolution' has put a potentially powerful tool in the hands of the manager.

The problem is that the technology is growing far faster than the related user skills. Managers are therefore faced with the question of how they are going to use this new tool. Software manufacturers may produce new packages for which major capabilities are claimed, but the speed with which such programs have to be produced to respond to technological change means that they are often poorly tested, if tested at all. The challenge to managers is to define precisely what extra information they can benefit from, and to ensure that any new system can be relied upon to produce that information.

Innovation   See *change*.

Inspection   See *quality control*.

Institute of Directors, The   This institute represents directors of all sizes of business. One of the services it offers is to keep a register of companies looking for funds and those interested in finding investments.

Insurance   There is a whole range of types of risk for an organization for which it is prudent for managers to arrange insurance cover. (For an example, see *product liability*.)

Insurance companies are experts at avoiding their responsibility to pay major claims, and the law gives them a powerful weapon with the stipulation that all insurance companies are *uberrimae fidei* (Latin for 'of the utmost good faith'). This means that the parties to an insurance contract must disclose all relevant information to the insurance company, otherwise the contract will not be binding. Thus managers must ensure that there is a written record that any circumstances affecting the insurance position of the business have been notified to the insurance company.

Internal Rate of Return   A method of *investment appraisal* (see separate entry). The internal rate of return is the percentage return earned over the life of a project on the cash invested in the project at any time. It is computed as the cost of capital rate at which *net present value* (see separate entry) is nil, and is subject to the same limitations as that method.

International Monetary Fund (IMF)   Set up at Bretton Woods (see separate entry) the IMF aimed to supervise the fixed exchange rate system. In a world of fluctuating exchange rates the IMF continues to promote international economic stability. Each member state subscribes quotas to the IMF and may borrow from the fund in times of economic difficulty. The IMF requires agreement on economic policies as a condition of drawings being made, the conditions becoming more stringent as drawings increase.

International Transport and Freight Forwarding   A competitive business where the margins are thin. The competition is primarily in terms of:

- the comprehensiveness of the network, both the geographic spread (continental, world-wide) and the variety of means (ships, planes and trucks); and

- speed – meaning speed of information transmission/documentation handling rather than the physical speed of vehicles, so it is all about documentation, know-how and computerization.

   It is also an industry in which there is a particular premium on being 'close to the customer'; knowing the customer's business and likely developments is the clue to seeing patterns/changes in the flow of goods, getting more business and knowing what business to keep out of.

Intrapreneurship   Within an established large organization the necessary bureaucratic procedures may have the drawback of stifling innovation. To get round this problem a 'new ventures' group may be set up independently of the rest of the organization to develop new projects and ideas. The aim of this 'intrapreneurship' is to allow new projects to be run in the fashion of the entrepreneur while being part of the established business. See also *skunk works*.

Intrinsic Rewards   Rewards deriving from the work itself, from its intrinsic interest, from understanding its contribution to a greater whole, from praise or recognition for good performance, or from the satisfaction of having done a good job (made a good deal, a wise decision, an inspired choice, or whatever). The implicit contrast is with extrinsic rewards, i.e., pay, fringe benefits, working conditions, etc. See also *Maslow's need hierarchy* and *hygiene factors and motivators*.

Investment Appraisal   A term which covers a variety of methods for deciding which projects to invest in. All investment appraisal involves making estimates about the future cash flows that will arise as a result of the project. Methods used include *payback, net present value* and *internal rate of return* (see separate entries).

J

Japan   The emergence of Japan as a major competitor in the 1970s and the dominance achieved by Japan in numerous industries, technologies and markets in the 1980s have made 'learning from Japan' an international industry. There is no shortage of things that differentiate the character and context of the Japanese company; indeed it has become a case of *embarras de richesse*. It may help, however, to group some of the points of interest/ difference:

- *Personnel policies*, such as life-time employment, security, strong allegiance to company, paternalistic provisions of company for employees – these considerations figured largely in the early Western accounts, but are no longer in the spotlight. They are also recognized as applying only to larger companies.

- *Technical ingenuity/inventiveness* (or imitative skills according to detractors) *backed by a strong engineering establishment*: engineering is regarded as a high status subject of study/career choice, with competitive entry to engineering courses at university and a predominance of managers who are engineers; Japan may be seen as the West Germany of the Far East.

- *Production is taken seriously*, marked by well-qualified production managers, well-trained foremen, a technically educated workforce, superior materials handling, and more attention to the minutiae of production methods and work organization; 'door to door, not floor to floor'; embracing the just-in-time supply method, quality circles and total quality control.

- *Differences of style and ethos*, such as consensual decision-making, a judicious blend of meritocracy and seniority, avoidance of the 'them-and-us' division between management and workers, management generalism, and a high and enduring commitment to team and company.

- *Institutional factors*, especially higher relative reliance on debt finance rather than on equity finance, the patience of Japanese banks, together with government support, MITI (Ministry of International Trade and Industry) and consensual industry–government relations.

- *Strategy*, taking a long-term view, export oriented and going for market share/market dominance rather than short-term margins; planning market entry, getting distribution system in place and having follow-up models in hand before launch of first model; persistence in the face of early difficulties, all leading to ultimate triumph.

Not surprisingly, all commentators have found something to admire and emulate in the Japanese system. A corollary need in the West is to know what they do badly, to find weaknesses competitors can exploit.

Job Rotation   A system for moving staff sideways into a different kind of job to enable employees to develop new skills, and also to give staff awareness of the needs of other parts of the business. It is particularly useful in preparing those who have specialized in one business function for a more general management role.

We know a company which not only operates a job rotation system but also insists that all new staff recruited for any aspect of management spend an initial year working as salesmen. They feel that this exposure to customers gives all managers a vital appreciation of customer needs.

Job Satisfaction   Workers derive job satisfaction from a wide range of factors that have been the subject of consideration by a number of writers. See *motivation*.

Job Sharing   A form of part-time employment whereby two people voluntarily share the responsibility of one full-time job. The job may be 'split' so that each employee does their part of the job independently, or 'shared' where a high degree of interaction is needed.

Job-sharing can be particularly attractive to women, offering part-time work in skilled and professional jobs where it might otherwise not be available. Employers can benefit from greater flexibility, increased cover in peak periods, availability of a wide range of skills in a job, and access to a wider employment pool.

Joint Ventures   Term used to describe the situation where two or more enterprises work together to exploit an opportunity. Joint ventures can involve partners with similar resources combining to undertake an activity which would be too large for them to undertake individually. More commonly the partners each have rather different resources to put into the venture. For example, licensing arrangements involve granting permission to other manufacturers to exploit the technical skills of an enterprise in exchange for a fee which, normally, is linked to sales. Thus one partner benefits from expanded sales of a product without the need to expand production capacity, while the other partner benefits from access to technical knowledge it does not itself possess. A common form of joint venture is *franchising* (see separate entry).

Just in Time   JIT is a system of organizing the flow of materials, components and bought-out parts into the production process pioneered by the Japanese. The idea is that these materials will arrive at the factory very shortly before they are needed for current production; they will not arrive too late thereby disrupting production, nor too soon thus incurring avoidable stockholding costs for the manufacturer, but just in time. The idea is simple; the challenge is in the organization and discipline to make it happen.

The discipline is presumed to be a Japanese cultural phenomenon, a matter of what is expected and regarded as important enough to make an effort for. On the organizational front it appears that JIT is often achieved by the large receiving company having a ring of component suppliers which are both geographically close and largely or wholly dependent on that one customer. The efficiency of some Japanese companies is a testimony to the advantages of JIT crossed with the suppliers' ring, though there may be less obvious social costs (see *vertical integration*).

L

Lawrence, P. and Lorsch, J.W.   Two American management academics, who are contingency theorists (see *contingency theory*) concerned with the relationship between the organization and its environment.

The essence of their theory is that increasing challenge from the environment – say more competition, advancing technology, changing consumer demand or whatever – will lead to an increasingly differentiated company structure in the sense of more discrete and specialized functions within the company (P. Lawrence and J.W. Lorsch, *Organization and Environment*, Harvard University Press, 1968). This in turn creates an internal company need for integration, the bringing together of these discrete functions and the bridging of the organizational gaps. And the final part of the Lawrence and Lorsch story is that in the sample of companies they studied the more commercially successful ones were those which handled the integration well.

This Lawrence and Lorsch study is vibrant with practical implications:

- If your company is facing more rather than less challenge, has it developed whatever specialized competence is necessary to handle the challenge?

- If it has, can it handle the integration (or is it just relying on the traditional method of co-ordination via hierarchy)?

See also *hierarchy* and *Burns, T.* for a British version of Lawrence and Lorsch.

Leadership Leadership and management are not the same, but they do overlap. They are not the same because:

- management jobs differ in the extent to which they require leadership – usually jobs in production management, sales management, general management and top positions put a higher premium on leadership skills than other jobs;

- some situations, such as crisis, turn-round or strategic change, put a higher premium on leadership than other situations;

- managers are usually required to do other things besides exercise leadership, e.g., control, organize, co-ordinate.

So what makes a good leader? There are several answers. The first answer is the trait approach to leadership, which asserts that good leaders are people with particular personality traits, say intelligence, confidence, initiative, ruthlessness, and so on. Or perhaps decisiveness, verbal skills, resolution, integrity, energy, maybe compassion. Here we have the first difficulty with the trait approach: there is no end to the list of desirable traits. What is more, some of them are hard to measure: intelligence is relatively easy, but what of compassion? And it is difficult to prove that people who have these traits are really more effective leaders than people who do not.

The second answer says leadership is about behaviour rather than traits, and this takes the pressure off measuring personality attributes. The numerous studies really throw up three behaviour dimensions, the first two of which are captured in Blake's grid:

- *task centredness*: the extent to which the task is taken seriously and rationally pursued;

- *people centredness*: the extent to which people are valued, motivated, cared for and well handled;

- *participativeness*: the extent to which colleagues/subordinates are involved in plans and decisions.

There is independent survey evidence to suggest that successful managers on the measure of achieved rank by age are participative, that is involve subordinates, and are perceived by subordinates as doing this. There is also evidence that individual managers who score high on both task centredness and people centredness, the two dimensions of Blake's grid, are above averagely successful in career terms (see *Blake's grid*). But this is to assume that the same strengths are relevant in all situations, an idea which is now rejected.

The third answer to the question what makes a good leader is thus more conditional. It suggests that good leadership is contingent on people and the situation. If we cross this idea of contingency with the three behaviour dimensions of task, people and participation, we can get some practical propositions:

- *Task centred leadership* is unsuitable where the task is naturally highly structured; task centred leadership is also inappropriate where the task is repetitive. But if the task is naturally unstructured, then task centred leadership tends to raise the satisfaction and performance of subordinates. Danger has the same effect – those involved in dangerous tasks tend to respond to task centred leaders, and subordinates who have authoritarian leanings prefer task centred leadership irrespective of the degree of danger, structuring and repetition.

- *People centred leadership* or supportive leadership tends to be effective with tasks that are stressful, frustrating or dissatisfying. In such cases supportive leadership may raise the subordinates' self-confidence and underline for them the importance of their contribution, with positive effects on morale. Again if the task is highly structured (boring, repetitive, little room for manoeuvre or expression of personal style) then supportive leadership is likely to raise satisfaction and performance (nothing else can!).

- *Participative leadership* is good for:

    (a) making subordinates well informed;

    (b) helping subordinates to balance the efforts–rewards equation;

    (c) getting subordinates more committed (to objectives they have more or less chosen through consensual decision-making);

    (d) giving subordinates more control over their work which is generally good for morale.

    What is more, when a task is both unstructured (poorly defined) and it appeals to subordinates (they want to succeed at it) then participative leadership raises satisfaction.

For a good discussion of leadership theories and application see Alan Bryman, *Leadership and Organizations* (Routledge and Kegan Paul, London, 1986).

See also *Hersey and Blanchard*.

Lead Time   The time it takes to make an item after the order is placed. It is important in understanding the causes of poor delivery performance, in that lead times are usually rather inflexible but manufacturers often commit themselves to undercutting these lead times – to get a sought-after order, to please a customer, because salesmen do not like to say no, and so on – thereby committing themselves to a subsequent delivery 'foul-up'.

See *delivery*.

Likert, Rensis   American management academic known for his four ideal organization types, known as System One, Two, Three and Four. They indicate a range of organizational types on an autocratic to participative continuum, where System One denotes an autocratic and authoritarian organization and System Four is a democratic and participative one.

Likert sees these four types as both indicating the general character of organizations and as having implications for individual management styles within organizations. He also provides rating scales to fix where any given organization/company comes on the System One–Four spread, and makes training recommendations on how to help move companies along towards Systems Three and Four, the democratic end of the spectrum (see Rensis Likert, *New Patterns of Management*, McGraw Hill, New York, 1961). Likert is very much a part of the *neo-human relations* movement (see separate entry) and is committed to the view that as organizations move in the System Three to System Four direction, morale goes up and the organization becomes more effective in that people work harder. The evidence on this issue is substantial but not unequivocal.

Finally, Rensis Likert is also the inventor of Likert scaling. A Likert scale is a summated scale in that responses can be totalled, and has as its objective to measure the degree of positive or negative effect. It is typically in the form of a proportion allowing the subject a range of responses from strongly disagree through to completely accept.

Limited Liability   Most countries have provision in their law for companies to be formed with 'limited liability'. This generally means that the directors and shareholders have no personal liability to pay the debts of the company, their personal liability being limited to an obligation to pay any amounts still owing for their own shares.

Banks and other financial institutions are well aware of this legal position, and when lending to a company with a small number of shareholders will normally require that they guarantee the loan repayment personally. Thus in practice the privilege of limited liability is less broad in its application than might at first appear.

Company law normally provides a range of safeguards against abuses of limited liability. In both the USA and the UK a manager offered a position as a company director would be well advised to ensure that the company is being run within the requirements of the law, since otherwise personal responsibility for the company's debts could arise.

Liquidation   The process of selling off all the assets of a company and paying out the proceeds. Where loans are secured by a fixed charge on specified assets then the sale proceeds of those assets are applied to meeting the claims of those specified lenders, any surplus cash being put into the pool of company resources to meet other claims. The proceeds of sale of all the assets not subject to a fixed charge are applied in order:

(a)   to pay liquidation costs;

(b)   to pay 'preferential' creditors (these are defined by law, mainly being government departments!);

(c)   paying creditors secured by a floating charge;

(d)   paying unsecured creditors;

(e)   any residue is shared by the shareholders as provided in the articles of association.

Liquidity   The availability of cash resources of an enterprise. A company is said to have 'liquidity problems' if there is difficulty in finding cash resources to meet obligations as they fall due.

See also *cash flow*.

Listed Company   A company with a full listing on the *Stock Exchange* (see separate entry).

M

Management Accounting   The role of the management accountant is to prepare and present accounting information in such a way as to help management formulate policies and plan and control the operations of the enterprise. This contrasts with the work of the financial accountant who prepares accounts for those outside the business. There are a number of differences between management accounts and financial accounts, including:

- Management control the content of the management accounts, which might include a wide range of different reports. For most enterprises the form of the financial accounts is laid down by law.

- Management accounts should contain information relevant for decision-making, based on estimates and valuations if necessary (see *cost* for an example of relevant information). Financial accounts must be objective and easily verifiable.

- Management accounts require a detailed analysis of income and expenditure. Financial accounts focus on the computation of profit.

- Management accounts must be prepared rapidly to enable managers to react to change promptly. Financial accounts must be more precise, but may be prepared over a longer period.

Management Buy-In   An arrangement, normally sponsored by a venture capital company, where a team of managers get together to find a company they can buy and run. The sort of manager involved is likely to be the kind who would opt for a *management buy-out* (see separate entry) given the chance.

Management Buy-Out   The purchase of a firm, or part of a firm, from the owners by members of the management team. The practice grew in the USA during the 1960s, and has developed in the UK since the second half of the 1970s. Where an organization decides to dispose of a division (see *divestment*) the existing management team may well appear as attractive purchasers.

Managers contemplating a buy-out can easily find expert professional advice on organizing and financing the arrangement. Often such advice can be arranged on a 'no deal, no fee' basis. More challenging to the manager in this position is the requirement to convert from a corporate mentality to an entrepreneurial mentality. (See *entrepreneur*.)

Management by Objectives (MBO) An approach to assessing performance by reference to the achievement of results rather than the performance of activities. Managers participate in the setting of individual objectives which are linked to overall objectives. The advantages of MBO are that activities become orientated to results avoiding the *activity trap* (see separate entry), objectives are clarified, managers become aware of the importance of their work, staff performance can be assessed, and morale may benefit from participation. On the other hand MBO can be a complex and costly process to implement. For example, it can be difficult to define a measurable unit of output that satisfactorily captures achievement of objectives. Thus the application of MBO has tended to be confined to large organizations.

Management Development Increasing the performance and experience of managers and enhancing their value to the company by career planning, performance appraisal and feedback, counselling and training.

Management Science The expression has two related meanings. First, management may be treated as a science – law-like, rational, predictable. This approach focuses on the decision, informed and rational, as the elemental management act. The second meaning is to denote a subject/course of study at university. Management science in this sense is different from business administration in that the former emphasizes the rational bases and quantitative components – operations research, statistics, mathematical modelling, decision analysis, and so on.

Management Style Most practitioners like the idea of management style, believe that they have one, that it is quite distinct and that there is nobody else quite like them. The fascination of the style idea indeed clearly derives from its association with individuality and choice. At the same time, it is beguiling in that there is no universally accepted definition or even approach.

Most of the literature on style is psycho-behavioural, exploring personality-linked dispositions and behaviours, and developing tests to measure these. At the same time, however, it has been variously argued that style is macro-cultural, that one can speak, for example, of a Latin American style; that it is national; that it is epochal in that styles change over time; that it can be redefined as leadership; and that it may be understood as a choice between activity sets, means to an end, or dimensions of jobs.

Given this lack of agreement and plethora of interpretation, is there anything managers can do to get a better understanding of their style and more out of it? There are at least three practical things.

First, the general rule is play your strengths and mask your weaknesses. But strengths can be overplayed, and weaknesses have to be dealt with – by compensation, delegation, partnership, corrective action, fail-safes, or whatever.

Second, it is worth doing some of the tests on offer from trainers and consultants; it will provide more substance to your image of yourself, and some of the tests offer guidance on the strengths and weaknesses of the propensities they reveal. The LIFO test, which reveals four basic management styles and their applications, is particularly to be recommended.

Third, most management jobs offer some choice. While there are always required performances, basic activities and constraints, there is usually some choice on a number of dimensions including:

- technical *v.* supervisory aspects of the job

- time spent with subordinates

- whether control or development of subordinates is emphasized

- innovation

- risk taking

- importance attached to boundary maintenance (protecting unit and subordinates)

There is a choice in the sense that one can attach more or less importance to these things, and to some extent do what one likes doing or does best. And the *de facto* choices made on dimensions such as these is a manifestation of style. The important thing is that the choices should be thought through and conscious. If you are strong on communication and motivating others, make sure you deploy this strength in the development of subordinates; if the control function leaves you cold but the job requires it, make sure (enough of) it is done some way.

Managerial Revolution   Term coined by James Burnham, author of *The Managerial Revolution* (John Day, New York, 1941), together with two other American academics, Berle and Means, who drew attention to the separation in the ownership and control of business companies. The idea is that shareholdings become dispersed and companies are run by professional managers, not by founder-owners. What these writers describe has largely come to hold for the majority of companies in most industrial countries. But if it is largely true, does it matter?

Certainly in the 1960s people thought that it did, that professional managers would espouse growth rather than profit maximization, thereby enlarging the management *cadres*. J.K. Galbraith in particular pushed the managerial revolution argument on a stage by arguing that large companies are run by 'the technostructure', an amalgam of senior managers and technical specialists, who will finance growth from retained earnings rather than increase dividend payments to shareholders.

Nearly half a century after Burnham's book the interpretation has changed. Professional managers, the good ones and the ones that survive, show themselves to be just as resolute at profit protection, profit maximization and financial control as any majority shareholder/entrepreneur. It may well be the case that economic climate is a more important determinant of top management posture than is the nitty-gritty of who owns what shares.

Managing Director   Most senior manager in a British company, key member of the board of directors, and equivalent of the American chief executive officer. He is often also chairman of the board of directors.

Manpower Planning   The overall plans for an enterprise will imply certain demands for manpower in the future. In a manpower planning exercise management consider the current manpower position in terms of skills, grades and locations, and compare this with the requirements of the corporate plan. If the business has a surplus of manpower for future needs then arrangements can be made to trim the workforce by 'natural wastage'. If extra manpower is going to be needed management can consider the labour market and decide whether it is going to be practical to recruit the extra staff – if not, the corporate plan may need to be changed. Manpower planning allows the enterprise to administer recruitment and training in a way that meets future needs rather than simply responding to current, and possibly short-term, requirements.

Manpower Services Commission (MSC)   A body set up in the UK under the Employment and Training Act 1973 to manage the government's employment and training services. The MSC offers a range of training services to employers, as well as being a source of trainees from a wide range of employers.

Manufacturing Policy   The background to the case for manufacturing policy is that most companies not only do not have one, but do not even think about manufacturing except with repugnance as a messy, noisy, dirty, unpredictable appendage to the head office.

But companies should develop a manufacturing policy, which:

- is conscious and thought out;

- recognizes that manufacturing is a competitive weapon for the company (not an unappetizing cost centre);

- that the principal aim is not necessarily cost and efficiency;

- that the equipment and process technology is variable, with varying implications for the company;

- so that trade-offs are required – one cannot have all the pluses with the same system.

In particular the choice of equipment and process technology involves trade-offs between:

- volume and flexibility

- speed and cost

- maintenance costs and down-time

- equipment renewal and down-time

- handling specials and cost

- short lines to suppliers/customers and cost of diseconomies of decentralized production

- cheap sites and availability of skilled workforce

Manufacturing policy needs to link manufacturing to corporate policy.

Market Capitalization   The value of a company implied by the market price of shares. Market capitalization is computed as:

Share price × Number of shares

It should be noted that this does not necessarily represent the amount for which a company could be bought or sold as a whole. A purchaser would probably have to bid substantially higher than the current market price to persuade the majority of shareholders to sell. Conversely, a seller of a large block of shares might well have to undercut the market price to find a buyer.

Marketing Concept   Term used to describe the view that a business should be *customer oriented* rather than *product oriented*. Put another way, the question 'what business are we in?' should be put regularly, and should be answered in terms of what customers buy rather than what the business produces.

The classic case often quoted is that of the railway companies. In the nineteenth century they came to dominate the transport business. In the twentieth century railways have declined even though the demand for transport has increased dramatically. It is argued that if the railway companies had been 'customer oriented' they would have identified themselves as being in the transport business, and would have involved themselves in the transport methods devised by twentieth century technology such as motor vehicles and aeroplanes. Being 'product oriented' the railway companies have declined in the face of competition which, in its initial stages, they did not even recognize.

Marketing Mix   Phrase coined by an American, J.N. Borden, in the 1960s. It summarizes the idea that companies do a variety of activities to market their goods and that the make-up of the 'mix' of activities varies with different companies, products and types of industry.

To take a simple example, the selling of goods will be affected both by their price and by their availability. One producer may charge a low price, but cut down on costs by requiring customers to collect goods from one of a small number of selling outlets; a rival producer may charge a higher price but spend more on offering customers the chance to collect goods from a far wider range of selling outlets. In this example each producer is aware of the influence of both price and availability of goods in the customer's decision to purchase, and each producer chooses a different 'mix' of these two features in selling their goods.

Various writers have put forward different ideas as to the ingredients that make up the 'marketing mix'. One of the most widely quoted is the *'Four Ps'* (see separate entry).

Marketing Research   The investigation into all aspects of how the output of a business is to be transferred to the consumer. It embraces consideration of:

- the market, considering what groups are consumers, trends in the size and nature of the market, and how that market is served;

- competitors, considering what products they offer, how those products are marketed, and potential new competitors;

- how consumers view products currently on offer;

- the range of advertising media appropriate to communicate the particular product to the consumer.

Research will be based on both 'primary data' collected specifically for a particular market research exercise, and 'secondary data' collected for some other purpose.

Market Segmentation   The market for a product can be analysed into 'segments' on which an enterprise may chose to focus. Ways of segmenting a market include:

- *geographical*, concentrating on a region which contains a high proportion of customers for a product;

- *demographic*, focusing on a particular age, class or sex group;

- *ethnic groups*, where it may be profitable to produce a product range appealing to the special traditions of a particular group;

- *psychographic segmentation*, using packaging and promotion to give a product an 'image' that appeals to a particular type of consumer – we know a paint manufacturer whose paint is produced in four different brand names. Retailers report that some customers refuse to accept an alternative brand when one runs out, even though the paint is identical;

- *personal taste* – in a market dominated by a 'standard' product there may be room for an alternative that appeals to a particular taste.

Maslow's Need Hierarchy   American psychologist Abraham Maslow has postulated a hierarchy of needs which people seek to satisfy. They are:

Meta	Self-actualization, fulfilment, doing what one can do best.
Ego	Pride, respect, power, independence, status.
Social	Love, friendship, belonging.
Security	Shelter, safety, saving.
Physiological	Air, food, water.

It is called a hierarchy because Maslow holds that man strives to satisfy each of these needs progressively from the bottom up, so that when physiological needs are taken care of attention focuses on security, and so on up the hierarchy.

Its relevance to management is three-fold:

(a)   In modern industrial societies the satisfaction of the higher order needs tends to be centred on work.

(b)   Part of Maslow's message is that relatively humble employees may also seek the satisfaction of ego and meta needs at work, and will be both happier and more effective if work is structured to allow them to do so.

(c)   There is subsequent research evidence (see *Blake's grid*) to suggest that successful managers are the ones whose personal emphasis is on the higher order needs.

Mass Production   Making a standardized product in large numbers, sometimes using assembly line methods. Mass production companies are generally believed to be more rather than less bureaucratic, to emphasize speed, organization and throughput, and in terms of Burns' theory to have a mechanistic rather than organic structure (see *bureaucracy*, *Burns* and *Woodward*).

It puts a premium on scale economies, control and the organization of supplies (see *just in time*). It also implies manufacturing for stock rather than for customer orders, and having a system of distributors/stockists in line with that – there is no point in making 1,000 cars a day if you have 'nowhere to put them'.

Master of Business Administration (MBA)   A postgraduate degree in the field of business and management awarded by many UK universities and a growing number of polytechnics. Some courses aim to cover a broad spread of management subjects, while others allow students to specialize heavily in particular subject areas; in addition, students are normally required to work on an individual, personally researched, project. Most full-time courses last one year, a few require two years. There are also a growing number of part-time MBA courses, based on day-release or evening teaching, and generally spreading over some three years.

There is a substantial degree of variation in the respect generally felt for MBAs from different institutions.

Materials Control   The department or function in industry concerned with organizing the supply of bought-out parts or materials needed for the company's manufacturing operation. Sometimes materials control is just an alternative to purchasing as an organizational entity (see *purchasing* and *production control*). But where the manufacture of products depends disproportionately on a large number of parts, then the control of production depends much more on lining up all the parts and materials on time than on scheduling itself. This may give rise to the following organization form:

Matrix Organization   This involves structuring a company in terms of two dimensions which criss-cross, say:

Function (e.g. sales, R & D, etc.)   ×   Product division

or

Function   ×   Geographic area

or

Area   ×   Product

On the positive side is that a matrix structure avoids the operational rigidities and restriction of decisional inputs associated with single-dimension structures *operating on a large scale*. At the same time it means people have double reporting lines (e.g., to the head of marketing and to the general manager for Canada) and live in an avowedly complex organizational milieu. It is a form for large companies, and professional managers who can practise restraint and organizational sensitivity.

Mediation   A mediator is a neutral party called in to assist in resolving a conflict. Unlike an arbitrator, a mediator is not given any authority to pass judgement. The role of the mediator is to make suggestions and recommendations to the two parties in dispute in order to help them reach an agreement.

See also *arbitration*.

Meetings Meetings are well known to be a standard part of the work of most managers, though there are some patterned variations. On the whole, the larger the company and the higher the individual's rank, the larger the proportion of time spent in formal meetings. Or to put it a little differently, there appears to be a line running from chief executive through general management and down the production management hierarchy, and all the positions on this line involve a significant amount of time spent in meetings, whereas there is more variation in the functional specialisms away from this line.

Meetings vary in content in a commonsensical way so that, for example, production managers discuss manning, hold-ups, schedules, production plans and scrap rates, while purchasing officers talk to design engineers about specifications and see suppliers' representatives. On the other hand, it is possible to classify meetings more analytically by function and purpose, distinguishing those that serve primarily the ends of:

- information exchange and co-ordination
- information exchange for control purposes
- problem-solving
- planning/devising future initiatives

though there may be some overlap between these types in practice.

Probably most managers in most countries complain (to anyone who is willing to listen) about the time they spend in meetings (though the loudest complainers are often the most avid prolongers of meetings). Indeed there usually is a case for a periodic review of the panoply of meetings in a company with a view to discarding any series which became institutionalized by accident or have outlived their usefulness.

More important is to see that existing meetings give 'value for money' within the normal constraints of time and human abilities, a responsibility especially for those initiating and chairing them. Apart from simple precepts such as:

- having the right people there;
- providing relevant information in advance;
- foreseeing obvious questions, not to obvert them but to offer satisfactory replies;
- letting everyone have their say, while 'keeping the ball in play';

probably the most important thing for the initiator is to define the purpose and ground rules, saying in effect what those taking part are there to do or decide according to what criteria, and then orchestrating individual contributions to that end.

Merger Term used when two companies are regarded as being combined rather than one acquiring the other. A merger has many of the potential benefits and dangers of an *acquisition* (see separate entry). However, with a merger there are likely to be especially sensitive problems in merging the corporate cultures of entities each of which is jealous of its own inheritance.

Methods In studies of management and business organizations there is a contrast, even a conflict, between the doing of in-depth studies of limited generality which are nevertheless rich in detail, and survey-style studies of large groups/numbers which are cheap and convenient but relatively shallow. Studies of the first kind are typically by interview or use observational methods, or are simply studies 'in depth' of particular cases; the work of *Carlson, Mintzberg* and *Stewart* in management research (see separate entries) are examples. An example of the second type of research is the *Aston Group* studies (see separate entry) and surveys of the background and qualifications of managers are also of this type.

In an ideal world researchers would be able to cross the two methods, but it is easier said than done.

Mintzberg, Henry Contemporary Canadian management writer best known for a study of the work of top managers (*The Nature of Management Work*, Harper & Row, New York, 1973). Mintzberg picks up the account of management work where Carlson (see separate entry) leaves off. That is to say, Mintzberg, like Carlson before him, documents the crowded, pressurized, hectic and non-contemplative nature of the work of senior managers, and indeed apostrophizes such work as marked by brevity, variety and fragmentation. But unlike Carlson, Mintzberg sees this as a natural state of affairs, not the product of disorganization or lack of policy. Even senior managers will have to fight fires (who else will?); it is right that they should deal with the unexpected and problematic, the obscure and unprogrammable: if the work were routine it would not need managers to do it!

Minutes Written record of a meeting or discussion, and generally useful as a reminder of what was decided (or was not) and who is going to do what. There are two things to watch: first, processing minutes can become a ritual: don't do it if it is not necessary; secondly, minute writing is an opportunity for political manipulation – if you cannot win the meeting, write the minutes.

Monopolies and Mergers Commission An agency set up by the UK government to identify abuses of monopoly power and to decide whether proposed mergers are likely to lead to a monopoly or a serious reduction in competition. The commission has the legal right to block mergers. In the

USA the Federal Trade Commission has a similar role, while the US 'anti-trust' laws are considerably more powerful than the equivalent UK legislation. This is an area where the *European Community* (see separate entry) is likely to develop an increasing interest.

Motivation   The process of influencing or stimulating a person to take action that will accomplish a desired goal. Traditionally managers have sought to motivate workers by a combination of rewards and penalties. However, a number of writers have identified a far more complex set of factors influencing motivation. See *appraisal, Argyris, compensation, complex man, expectancy theory, Hersey and Blanchard, Herzberg, human relations, hygiene factors and motivation, leadership, Likert, Maslow's need hierarchy, neo-human relations, organizational behaviour, participation, path goal theory* and *Theory X and Theory Y.*

Multinationals   A firm engaged in business in two or more countries may be referred to as a multinational company (MNC). Some authorities argue that the term multinational should be more narrowly defined, involving operations in a number of countries, a substantial proportion of assets abroad and a global management orientation.

This type of enterprise offers a special challenge to managers. The MNC has to cope not only with the economic, political, legal and social environment of the domestic country but also of each country in which it operates. Managers exchanged between countries have to adapt their approach to a new environment. For example, a manager from the USA might find himself confronted with a workforce in another country where the law does not allow any employee to be dismissed. More subtle cultural differences also arise. For example, a manager from the USA might give instructions for a foreign employee in broad terms, believing that he is showing respect for that employee's ability to show initiative; the foreign employee, in some cultures, might feel aggrieved at what would be regarded as an imprecise brief. Thus successful management in the MNC involves an understanding of the cultural environment in each country where the enterprise operates.

N

Naked Market   Phrase coined by British management guru Robert Heller, and title of one of his books (*The Naked Market*, Sidgwick & Jackson, London, 1984). The idea is that all companies stand naked before the demands of the market, which they must profitably satisfy or go under.

The negative aspect of the thesis is that there has been an erosion of the forces that used to protect some companies – reputation, tradition, inertia, national barriers, monopolism and tariff policy. At the same time, cheaper and more flexible new technologies, containerization and swifter transport, have lowered market *entry barriers* (see separate entry).

The result, crossed with the early 1980s recession and heightened competition, is that everyone is invading everyone else's market. Nothing is safe, and every market share has to be defended – by attack.

National Culture   The idea of national culture was discredited in the 1930s and 1940s by its association with various totalitarian regimes. In the quarter of a century after the Second World War, a period marked by reconstruction, prosperity and growth, the assumption was that there were no interesting or significant differences between countries likely to impinge on their economic performance or management structures. Indeed, social scientists posited the notion of convergence theory, which suggested that industrialism had its own logic and dynamic such as to eliminate progressively differences between advanced industrial countries.

The 1970s, however, saw a new interest in the differences between countries, even between advanced industrial countries which are also parliamentary democracies, giving rise to a series of cross-cultural and comparative studies in economics and management. In Britain this movement was fuelled by a recognition of relative economic under-performance, and a search for causes which often explored in a comparative way social and cultural determinants of national economic performance.

Today it is generally recognized that many management phenomena vary on a country-to-country basis, including:

- management style, where broad national styles transcend individual differences;

- attitudes to work, both simple things such as importance attached to work, and more subtle variations including willingness to accept power differences in industrial organizations or ability to cope with uncertainty;

- organization structure, and indeed there are tightly controlled studies showing systematic differences in company structure between Britain, France and West Germany;

- the relative status in companies of functions such as sales, finance, production and engineering;

- the nature and purpose of control in companies;

- broad strategy differences, such as the French emphasis on growth, the American on profitability, and the German corporate penchant for technical quality rather than business policy.

Neo-Human Relations   This is a rather loose phrase applied to the post-war developments in motivation theory, following on from the Hawthorne based *human relations* movement (see separate entry). Researchers, consultants and trainers in this school emphasize the non-material rewards, incentives and human needs that may be satisfied at work. The key names in this school are Abraham Maslow, Douglas McGregor, Chris Argyris and Frederick Herzberg. See *Hygiene factors and motivators*, *Maslow's need hierarchy* and *Theory X and Theory Y*.

Netherlands Holland is such 'a clean well-lighted place' where 'everyone speaks English' that British and Americans who have business dealings with the Dutch tend to think there is nothing they need to know. This is not so:

- The Dutch take contractual obligations very seriously.

- They have a liking for factual accuracy and being in the right; getting the date wrong in Groningen will lose you much more credibility than in Chicago.

- They are strong on anti-bribery and corruption (and relish the belief that no one else is).

- Dutch people dislike displays of individual difference – cleverness, striving, achievement – and think them in bad taste; they may tolerate it from foreigners but are unlikely to engage in it themselves to please foreigners.

- The Dutch are strong on emotional control and restraint; they make the industrial democracy machinery work, cope with two-tier boards, 'make-out' in multinationals with matrix structures, and thrive on complicated wage negotiations.

- The Dutch as professional/managerial employees want different things (from their Anglo-Saxon counterparts); they are less motivated by money (having high marginal tax rates) and less ambitious for corporate advancement but more motivated by conditions, training opportunities and intrinsic job interest.

Although the Netherlands is smaller than Lake Michigan, the Dutch have a very strong sense of regional differences, reinforced by traditional religious differences. It is a good thing for business visitors to be sensitive to this.

Net Present Value (NPV) A sophisticated method of *investment appraisal* (see separate entry). For any proposed project net present value is found in two stages:

(a) Estimate the net cash flows, including the initial investment, which are expected to arise in each year.

(b) For each year 'discount' the cash flows to their 'present value'. For this purpose we need to assume a 'cost of capital', being the percentage rate that a company is assumed to be paying for the funds it employs. We can then calculate a 'discount factor' by using special tables.

In principle a business should embark on any project with a positive net present value. If forced to choose between projects then the business should opt for that with the highest NPV.

This is a highly sophisticated method which can be demonstrated to maximize the value of the business if applied properly. The problem is that it depends on the reliability of both the forecasts of future cash flows and the 'cost of capital' figure. In practice many managers prefer the simplicity of the *payback* method (see separate entry).

Networking   This is a particular and sophisticated version of outworking (see *outworker*) in the software industry. Trained professionals engaged in programming or systems design work at home, checking into a central office periodically, or being visited/contacted by an organizer to check on progress and integrate contributions to a project. Networking is also a special case of flexible working hours.

Non-Executive Director   Member of a board of directors who is not a full-time salaried manager in the enterprise concerned. The involvement of the non-executive director is typically restricted to attendance at board meetings and preparation therefor. Their value is held to be in the outsider's objectivity they can bring to bear, plus the fact that unlike many executive directors, they are not lobbying for the interests of a particular function.

There is a lot of variation from country to country in the sort of people who are appointed to non-executive directorships. In Sweden it tends to be senior managers from other companies; in West Germany, representatives of major customers, suppliers and the banks; in Britain there is a penchant for the status-lending director (i.e., someone with a landed title, retired admiral, etc.) and for 'wise old birds in the City'.

O

Objectives   Desired future states of affairs that a company is aiming at. Objectives should be the product of strategic consideration, should determine the allocation of resources, and provide standards against which performance – corporate, divisional, and individual – may be assessed. See also *corporate strategy* and *priorities*.

One Minute Manager   *The One Minute Manager* is the snappy title of a best-selling book by American academic turned entrepreneur, Kenneth Blanchard (Spencer Johnson co-author, Fontana Paperbacks, London, 1983).

The message is: have good objectives and reinforce them. Each manager should have a short, sharp list of goals on one side of a sheet of paper, readable within a minute. Achievement or non-achievement should be followed by short, sharp 'praisings' or 'blamings', all within a minute.

Open-Plan The open-plan office has been claimed to save up to 33% of the space taken up by traditional individual offices, as well as cutting maintenance and cleaning costs. Other benefits claimed include greater flexibility, easier communication and closer supervision.

Research has identified some drawbacks, however. These include a tendency for management to become more involved in routine matters. Problems can also arise from demotivation of staff through the loss of the status symbol of the individual office.

Open System In *socio-technical systems theory* (see separate entry) an open system is one that has an exchange relationship with its environment, whereas a closed system does not. It is a useful distinction because organizations or parts thereof are often treated as closed systems (self-contained, self-sufficient) when in fact they are open.

Organizational Behaviour A major sub-discipline of the study of management, concentrating on people, their behaviour in organizations, and on the non-financial and non-technical aspects of companies generally. Key issues in organizational behaviour include:

- goal setting
- organizational structure and its determinants
- *organization design*
- effect of technology
- *motivation*
- *job satisfaction*
- morale
- *leadership*

See separate entries as appropriate.

Organizational Development (OD) OD has two roots. The first is *socio-technical systems theory* (see separate entry), the idea that work units are simultaneously a social system and a technical system and that the art of job design is to have them converge. The second is the *neo-human relations* ideas on self-actualization and job enrichment (see separate entry), which came to be reformulated in the 1970s as quality of working life (QWL). So the purpose of OD is to raise the QWL and at the same time OD specialists believe this will enhance organizational effectiveness and performance. In practice this is achieved by tinkering with the social and technical systems, often attempting to build in more variety, autonomy, self-supervision, job enlargement, and so on.

Another common strand running through OD consultancy in practice is the idea that one brings conflicts into the open in order to solve them: this technique has produced some spectacular successes, but it does not always work! It has been said that an OD consultant is to the organization what the psychotherapist is to the individual – he can help if help is wanted.

Organization Chart   A chart which tries to record the formal relationships within an organization, showing the main lines of communication and the flow of authority and responsibility through the management hierarchy. Such charts help management define organizational relationships and provide information for those, such as new personnel, who need an introduction to the enterprise.

In drawing up organization charts, certain dangers need to be borne in mind. They can introduce rigidity into the organizational structure, and they can cause problems in defining closely status issues which might be better left ambiguous. They also become out of date rapidly as the management structure adapts and managers change roles. Thus the organization chart can be a dangerous tool unless management are prepared to incur the costs of careful drafting and regular updating to avoid these problems.

Organization Design   A management discipline which addresses the question: what should the structure of an organization be? The practical issues covered include the shaping in organizational terms of the jobs which people do, degrees of definition and specialization of tasks, organizational shape including the question of the tall and squat triangles produced by varying the hierarchy and the span of control (e.g., long hierarchy × small span of control = tall, slender triangle, and vice versa), centralization *v.* decentralization, functional *v.* divisional organization, and so on.

The contingency approach is central to ideas on organization design (see *contingency theory*), that is, the idea that there is no 'one best design' for all organizations but that the most appropriate design varies according to the organizational objectives, technology, stage of development and type of environment (see *Aston Group*, *Burns*, *Lawrence and Lorsch* and *Woodward*).

Among the researches on organization structure, the work of Lawrence and Lorsch is a landmark in that it demonstrates the need for organizations in turbulent environments to develop greater differentiation (special sub-units to deal with particular contingencies) which in turn gives rise to a need for greater integration – notoriously difficult to achieve, both aspects being essential for operating success.

A lot of interesting and practical ideas have come out of the organization design researches, but if there is a limitation it is that organizations are not usually 'greenfield sites' with regard to design, much of which is given. This means that applying organization design ideas is to engage in organizational change which is in turn a political process.

Organization Man   Title of a popular management book in the 1950s by journalist William H. Whyte (Simon & Schuster, New York, 1956). Whyte's thesis is that by the 1950s the earlier generation of thrusting, entrepreneurial managers had been replaced in the USA by a bunch of organizational yes-men. This prototypical organization man lacks independence, originality and drive, but he is kindly, courteous, co-operative, loyal to the corporation and strongly committed to group membership and group decision-making. It is a very readable book, and one that clearly captured a mood.

The book is now widely regarded as 'a period piece'. What is more, Whyte's treatment of the American corporation in the 1950s is far from even-handed, underlining the weaknesses and ignoring the strengths (the period was after all one of substantial corporate growth and prosperity). There is, however, a practical and valid message: corporations need individuals, leadership and entrepreneurialism, no matter how large and apparently stable.

Outworker   Term originating in British economic history to denote the domestic system of industry (woollen textiles) in the eighteenth century, where organizers took raw materials to outworkers, who made up the final products in their homes. The term has come back into use to denote precisely the same phenomenon, workers engaged in their own homes on knitting, sewing and finishing jobs on clothes. The smaller and more specialist end of the British textile industry is organized in this way. Using outworkers is also a standard device for business start-ups in textiles, where the entrepreneur cannot or will not fund the cost of machinery and premises at the outset.

Overtime   Time worked beyond the normal working hours, typically by hourly paid blue-collar workers, at higher hourly rates. In theory, overtime is a management resource, something that can be 'turned on' at a price if there is a upturn in orders or to clear a backlog. In practice, it tends to become institutionalized, with regular overtime working regarded as a standard supplement to basic pay. This restricts management's options, and affects productivity calculations.

P

Parkinson, C. Northcote   English writer and academic best known for Parkinson's Law, which states that work will expand to fill the time available for its completion (*Parkinson's Law and the Pursuit of Progress*, John Murray, London, 1958). More generally Parkinson's name is associated with the critique of bureaucracy and especially the stern warning that unless checked bureaucracy will grow, with strangulating effect. The business implication is that it pays in both senses to keep a watch on the size and power of the headquarters staff and, indeed, of central formations and staff units generally.

Participation   The name given to any attempt to involve employees in organizational decision-making, though it is probably best to distinguish between the American and European versions. In the American view, participation is anything which improves the individual's ability to determine his own fate within an (employing) organization. In practice American participation tends to be focused on 'the coal face', on the worker doing his job and decisions bearing directly on how this job is done. Concomitantly both people centred and participative supervisory styles have been favoured in the USA, at least in the 1960s and 1970s. The European view of participation, on the other hand, is more institutional, and suffused by the idea of employee involvement in/contribution to corporate strategy and policy-making. In practice it leads to industrial democracy and co-determination, with institutions such as the works council and employee representation on the board of directors: *West Germany*, *Sweden* and the *Netherlands* are three European countries with co-determination systems (see separate entries).

Participation has been widely viewed as leading to both heightened job satisfaction and better performance. The evidence, however, is not entirely convincing, though there is strong evidence of an association between a participative management style and career success (see *leadership*).

Path Goal Theory   Theory based on an expectancy view of work motivation, where expectancy theorists say people choose the levels of effort at which they are prepared to work. What is more, choosing a high level of effort is contingent upon the individual believing:

- high effort will lead to good performance;

- good performance in turn will lead to benefits for the individual.

The theory is important in calling into doubt the conventional assumption that people, or at least professional and managerial employees, will 'naturally' engage in a high level of effort. In practice they may not if it looks to them like striving for the impossible, or if they doubt the organization's ability to reward them even if they achieve the impossible. See also *expectancy theory*.

Payback   The payback period is the length of time it is expected to take for the net cash inflows from a new project to cover the original capital investment. Many companies use the payback method to decide between projects for investment. The method has the following advantages:

- It is simple to use and understand.

- It is based on the most easily predicted cash flows, i.e., those in the near future.

- Since payback involves choice of the project with the shortest payback period, it restricts the time cash is tied up in projects and so helps *cash flow* (see separate entry).

On the other hand, critics argue that payback is a crude measure, ignoring the amounts of cash flows after the end of the payback period.

See also *investment appraisal*.

Pendulum Arbitration Traditionally industrial disputes have been embittered by each party adopting an initial extreme position in order to have ample room for negotiation. Pendulum arbitration is a device to prevent this. Each party to a dispute puts their proposed solution to an arbitrator who must choose either one solution or the other, without compromise between the two. Thus each party to the dispute has an incentive to moderate their claim to the point where their solution is likely to appeal to the arbitrator as the most moderate.

Personal Skills The early management literature treated personal or social skills in a residual way (see *classical management* and *Fayol*), but more recent research and practitioner testimony have emphasized their importance. The relevance is to the ability to build and sustain relationships, motivate and communicate, and get some of it right by intuition rather than powers of analysis.

Personnel The role of the personnel manager is to provide for the acquisition, maintenance and utilization of an organization's human resources. This role embraces a range of functions such as recruitment, selection, training, career planning, wage and salary administration, *manpower planning* (see separate entry) and labour relations. Personnel managers may also be involved in developing the organization structure. There is a growing trend for the personnel department to be involved with organizing management development programmes, one result of which can be an enhanced status among other managers.

The personnel manager can face a difficult conflict between two aspects of this role. On the other hand, in the pursuit of productivity the personnel department will be involved in monitoring the performance of workers. On the other hand, the personnel manager has a responsibility for each worker's long-term career development, and this may conflict with immediate productivity objectives. Put crudely, the personnel manager must represent the objectives of the organization to the workforce and the objectives of the workers to the organization.

Personnel Audit An 'audit' of the personnel function can serve three basic purposes:

(a) To ensure that sound personnel policies are being carried out. Thus any erosion of standards can be detected before a crisis arises.

(b) To evaluate the costs and benefits of alternative personnel procedures. Most personnel objectives can be achieved in a variety of ways. For example, if the organization needs more highly qualified staff then money can be spent either on recruitment from outside or on training existing staff. Thus it is desirable to review periodically the cost effectiveness of the methods used.

PLURALISM

(c) To identify new challenges to the organization calling for a revision of personnel policies.

Peter, Lawrence J. (1919–) Originator of the 'Peter Principle' that 'In a hierarchy every employee tends to rise to his level of incompetence.' This is based on the observation that an employee who performs a job efficiently tends to be promoted to a new, more senior, job in the hierarchy. When the employee reaches a job which he cannot do well, then it is unlikely that further promotion will follow. The employee is unlikely to be dismissed, because of legal and trade union restrictions on unfair dismissal, and also because those more senior in the hierarchy will not wish to admit that the promotion they have authorized has proved to be a mistake. Thus the employee is left stranded at the 'level of incompetence', to the discomfort of the employee and the detriment of the organization.

Dr Peter based his principle, initially, on observation of the North American educational system during his career as an academic. His satirical style of writing makes his works eminently readable, but may have resulted in his observations being taken less seriously than they deserve. Many organizations have noted the Peter principle, responding in two ways:

(a) Rigorous consideration of the qualities an employee will require in a new job, and assessment of whether the employee possesses the new qualities needed in addition to those already demonstrated.

(b) Structuring the hierarchy in such a way as to make it possible to transfer an employee who has been unsuccessful in a new post back to the field where achievement was first displayed.

Pluralism In general sociology the term pluralism is used to suggest that there are a variety of countervailing forces and disparate interests in society, and that they roughly balance each other out so that society is not actually torn apart.

At a more specific level the term has also come to be applied to the understanding of formal organizations in terms of the disparate interests within groups, functions and individuals. The pluralistic approach to the understanding of companies thus recognizes:

- the difference of interest between capital and labour, and a shifting accommodation between them;
- different policy preferences within 'the ruling coalition' (= top management/people of influence in the company);
- the different interests and objectives of the various functions/departments;
- the fact that individuals may well be following 'war aims' which take priority over company objectives.

Thus a pluralistic approach seeks to understand the *variety* of forces and interests, together with their resolution and outcome.

See *political approach*.

Political Approach A limitation of some theories of leadership and motivation is that they tend to overlook the existence within organizations of individuals and groups pursuing different interests. The political approach has grown up as a counterpoise to this element of blandness in the organizational behaviour literature: this approach takes as its starting point individuals acting singly or in coalition to try to achieve the things they want; it sees the individual as proactive and wilful, and eschews semi-abstractions of the 'for the good of the company' and 'all pulling together' type. It deals in terms of power and influence, conflict and coalition. For a sustained exposition of this approach see: Robert Lee and Peter Lawrence, *Organizational Behaviour: Politics at Work* (Hutchinson Educational, London, 1985).

POSDCORB Mnemonic propounded by Luther Gulick, management writer/consultant and one-time member of President Roosevelt's three-man Administrative Management Committee, to denote the function/responsibility of top management. The letters stand for:

- Planning
- Organizing
- Staffing
- Directing
- Co-ordination
- Reporting
- Budgeting

POSDCORB is one in a series of semi-abstract formulations of the purpose/function of higher management starting with Henri Fayol in the First World War period (see *Fayol* and *classical management*).

Power A key variable in the analysis of companies/organizations. It is what makes things happen. Its strength and direction, together with the counterforces and obstacles in its way, determine the direction companies take and chart the course of events in the lives of individuals.

A focal point for organizational behaviour literature on power is to make clear the *different* bases on which power may rest, which include:

- *Reward power*: the ability to give people things they want, or at least 'use your influence' to make this more likely.

- *Coercive power*: the converse of reward power, it is the stick rather than the carrot; coercive power is the ability to discipline, punish, burden or disadvantage people.

- *Legitimate power*: the acceptance by those being influenced of the right of the powerholder; subordinates may obey a supervisor because they believe he is the one who should tell them what to do irrespective of his ability to reward or coerce. Thus legitimate power is similar to the classical idea of authority, except that it does not come from the top down, but is given by the subordinates, and of course it is always possible that the subordinates give legitimate power to someone other than a formal superior.

- *Referent power*: based on people identifying with powerholders, responding to their feeling that this is the way he should act and that they would act in the same way if they were him.

- *Expert power*: based on special abilities or knowledge, so that a manager may be obeyed because of respect for his technical know-how. It is the classic power base for managers in staff/specialist functions with regard to their colleagues in other departments or general management.

It is important to understand that there are varieties of power base because:

- it means one is following different people for different reasons;
- the counterplays vary with the powerbase;
- there is seldom an exact overlap between the distribution of (various kinds of) power and the formal authority positions in a company.

See also *authority*.

Preventive Maintenance Servicing or refurbishing plant and equipment on a regular and scheduled basis, not reactively in response to breakdowns. The case for preventive maintenance is that it reduces uncertainty: you know when the 'down-time' is going to be because of the schedule, and breakdowns become less likely. Not generally a British strength.

Price Setting a price for the output of a business is one of the most important, and difficult, management decisions. Considerations to be taken into account include:

- *Attitudes of customers*. Generally one would expect that demand for output would increase as prices are reduced, but this is not always the case. For some goods a high price acts as a 'signal of quality' to the buyer. This obviously applies to fashion goods, such as clothes and perfume. The same principle can sometimes apply in other cases. In one example a commercial vehicle producer found that an increase in price led to increased demand, because the vehicles were perceived by buyers to be of higher quality.

- *Behaviour of competitors.* The amount that the business is able to charge is strongly influenced by the prices set by competitors. For many years one of the UK's largest motor manufacturers did not produce a car in the smallest range, because a major competitor was selling their small car so cheaply that a rival could not be produced at a comparable price.

- The price that can be charged for a product will also depend on the *accompanying level of service* provided.

- A business may be subject to *legal or trade restrictions* on pricing policies. For example, in the UK lawyers are not allowed to charge for their services on a 'contingency' basis, whereby the amount of their fee depends on the outcome of litigation; the reason for this restriction is to safeguard the integrity of the legal profession.

- Prices have to be set at a level where costs will be covered, so that the *costs of the business* will affect pricing policies.

These examples illustrate the variety of factors influencing the pricing decision.

Price Analysis   This is a practice sometimes adopted by companies to assist them in their sourcing arrangements and negotiations with suppliers. Its essence is to calculate precisely and realistically the cost of an item the company doing the analysis wishes to buy from a supplier. This knowledge may then inform negotiations with potential suppliers. It is not just a case of powerful buyers intimidating defenceless suppliers (though it happens), but sometimes of helping potential suppliers to improve the efficiency of their costing and manufacturing methods.

Price Earnings (P/E) Ratio   A widely quoted ratio for listed companies, computed as:

$$\frac{[\text{Share price}]}{\text{Earnings per share}}$$

The ratio links the earnings (i.e., profit) figure shown in the accounts with the current share price. It is interesting because it indicates how the stock market views the prospects of the company. A low P/E ratio suggests a belief that profits will drop in the future; a high P/E ratio indicates a confidence that profits will rise. While managers may regard a high P/E ratio as an indication of public confidence in their company, it does carry a corresponding challenge to match these expectations.

Priorities   The idea of priorities operates at various levels. At the highest level the reference is to the setting of company objectives and, if necessary, ordering them in importance or urgency with corresponding implications for resource allocation (see *corporate strategy*). In manufacturing, priorities have a production control significance (see *production control* and *production planning*), referring to the time sequence or order in which particular jobs are required by customers. Finally, in terms of personal time management, priorities are either the things you do first, or the things that are most important. A lot of management jobs are pressured and fragmented, and it may help to come to the office with a very short list of priorities to be achieved or progressed on any given day, other accomplishments being treated as a bonus.

Problem Child   Term used by the *Boston Consulting Group* (see separate entry) to describe a product where the company has a low market share yet there is a good growth rate. It is argued that a decision has to be made either to invest in such a product to improve market share or drop it altogether.

Problem-Solving   Sometimes regarded as a manager's basic task. Stages in problem-solving might include:

- *Recognize the problem* – managers should give some part of their time to identifying opportunities to make decisions.

- *Define the problem* by reference to the causes rather than the symptoms. For example, we might recognize a problem with a business from the symptom of poor profit. In order to define the problem, we have to identify a cause, such as poor stock control.

- *Consider a range of alternatives* to solve the problem. *Brainstorming* (see separate entry) can help us broaden our range.

- *Evaluate our alternatives*, considering the full range of effects of each alternative. For example, if one solution to our problem of 'poor stock control' is to cut stock levels, we must consider the effect on costs of smaller purchase quantities, the effect on production of higher risks of running out of stock, and the effect on sales of a higher risk of not achieving prompt delivery.

- *Choose and implement a solution* – the manager must make sure that those responsible actually carry out the decision.

- *Evaluate the decision*, considering in the light of experience how the solution could be improved. This may lead to further improvement, and is also an important part of the manager's own self-development.

Process Production   The preparation of dimensional products. A dimensional product is one that has to be weighed or measured, as opposed to integral products which may be simply counted – cars, coat-hangers and capstan lathes are integral, but kilowatt hours of electricity, cubic feet of liquid oxygen and tons of nitrate fertilizer (even when in sacks!) are dimensional. In practice the process industries are chemicals, pharmaceuticals, petroleum, brewing, food processing and energy.

97

Production Control   The department or function in industry which devises and monitors a production schedule, that is, it decides what jobs will be done (items manufactured) in what order, in what numbers (batch sizes) and in which time deadlines – and then tries to make it happen. See also *production planning*.

Production Engineering   The department that comes between *design* or *research and development* on the one hand (see separate entries) and production on the other. Design will bring a product or component to prototype stage, and production engineering will take over and devise methods for its manufacture in the required numbers. Production engineering is also charged with solving any technical problems in production, and in the engineering industry will run a tool room for making up jigs, fixtures and other aids to manufacturing. In Britain initiative for machinery/equipment renewal usually comes from the production engineering department. In industries with a dimensional product it may be called process engineering (see *process production*).

Production Planning   The department or function in industry concerned with the planning of output over time. In contradistinction to *production control* (see separate entry) which is concerned with the implementation of a production schedule, production planning may have two meanings:

(a)   Production planning and production control may be two acts of the same play, where planning is about middle-term intentions and control about short-term performance.

(b)   In process industries (see *process production*) where output is determined by system adjustments the important thing is to plan production in the light of anticipated demands, so that planning is critical and control is marginal and does not appear on the organization chart.

Productivity   Productivity is a measure of *efficiency* (see separate entry), measured by the ratio of some unit of output to some unit of input. Suppose that last week we produced 440 widgets in 40 hours and this week we have produced 500 widgets in 50 hours, in this example production has gone up by 60 widgets but productivity has gone down from 11 widgets per hour (440/40) to 10 widgets per hour (500/50).

The term productivity is most commonly used in relation to inputs of labour, but productivity data needs to be interpreted with some care. For example, low production per hour worked may be attributable to poor machinery rather than poor handling of labour. Nevertheless, labour productivity is frequently used as a measure of a manager's success in handling employees.

Product Liability   If a consumer suffers loss or damage as a result of some defect in a product, then the legal claim for compensation is known as product liability. In the USA a leading manufacturer of farm machinery pays premiums for insurance against such claims amounting to some 7% of sales. In Europe the law tends to give consumers less protection and lower damages, but a recent EEC directive due to be implemented by the end of 1988 points towards greater burdens on manufacturers.

Managers would therefore be well advised to consider carefully whether the business is fully insured in this area. Managers may also be able to reduce potential liabilities. For example, under the new European Community directive liability will be placed on the producer rather than the retailer, *except* where a retailer adopts the product by putting their own brand on it. Thus retail managers may move away from 'own-brand' labels in response to the new law.

Profit The profit and loss account, normally published annually, reports on the income and expenditure of a business during a period of time, the difference between the two being 'profit' (or 'loss'). Profit offers an apparently objective measure of the extent of management's success in running the business. However, there are a number of reasons why the profit measure should be used with some care:

- There are a large number of technical complexities in the way accountants compute profit involving a choice between equally justifiable treatments. Thus by 'creative accounting' the profit figure can be artificially boosted or depressed.

- The conventions by which accountants try to impose some objectivity in the computation of profit are sometimes economically unrealistic. For example, the training costs of a business will, in practice, be expected to yield future benefits, but will be written off as an expense in the year training actually occurs. Thus if management cut down on training activities they may well boost the current year's profit figure, even though their action might be damaging to the business in the long term.

- Increases in trading activity may well lead to increased reported profit, but in the short term lead to outflows of cash to finance the expansion. If the financial requirements for expansion have not been properly planned for, then this can lead the business into financial difficulties (see *cash flow*).

- In some cases a trading activity may be designed to meet some non-financial objective – this applies to many public sector organizations. In such cases profit is incomplete as a measure of management achievement.

Thus managers should use profit as a measure of achievement with some care, while at the same time being aware that in practice they will often be judged on their reported profit figures.

Program Evaluation and Review Technique (PERT)   A particular technique for applying *critical path analysis* (see separate entry) which became well known when it was applied to the Polaris programme.

Promotion   The whole range of methods available for communicating with customers and potential customers, involving both the presentation of information and persuasion to buy the product. In promoting a product we have to consider such issues as:

- *Who are our customers, and which of their needs are we trying to satisfy?* It is not always easy to define which decision-maker has most influence on the decision to purchase a product. For example, husbands and wives may be influenced by rather different considerations in the purchase of a family car.

- *What does our product provide, what facts must be provided to demonstrate this, and what emotions must we appeal to?*

- *How can we best communicate our message to our customers?* Possible methods include personal selling, advertising, sales literature and other materials, sales promotion and public relations. The balance between these methods is sometimes called the 'promotional mix'.

- *What do we need to communicate to the various parts of the distribution chain, and how can we best do this?* Those in the different levels of the distribution chain will have interests in matters other than those which concern the ultimate consumer. For example, retailers will be very interested in the profit margins they can earn on the sale of a product.

Public Relations (PR)   PR is about handling a company's relations with society, especially in respect of sustaining its (hopefully) favourable image. PR may be carried out in two ways: by independent PR firms which offer their services to corporate clients on a fee basis like, say, advertising agencies, or by a company's own PR or public affairs department.

The jocular cynicism with which the PR function is popularly regarded is in part unjustified. PR people are often more sensitive to moral issues and social evaluations than are executives generally, if only because they know they will be in the front line if the company is 'caught in the act'. Neither is the PR function invariably reactive, in the sense of responding to crises or attacks on the company's standing: PR may well be proactive in taking measures to promote a company's standing, and an in-company PR department may engage in the development of socially responsible corporate policies where none existed before.

The attactions of PR work are considerable. Apart from the glamour associated with the media and being in the public eye, PR work involves contact with top management, exposure to sensitive information, affords an overview of the company's operations and is a most challenging job in terms of managing upwards.

Puppy dog close   Even when the salesman is making a positive impression on potential customers, to actually finalize the deal it is still necessary to overcome the natural human reluctance to make a decision, commit resources and preclude other options. This basic fact is well recognized and has led to the development of a number of 'closes' (see *close*) to get customers to 'sign the order form'. One of them, the puppy-dog close, operates on a pet shop analogy. It involves the salesman/shop assistant suggesting to the potential customer that he should 'hold the puppy'. The puppy, of course, snuggles down against the customer and looks up so appealingly that he can never be relinquished. The moral is: if the goods are that good, let the customer take them off and play with them – they will never be returned.

Purchasing   The department or function of a manufacturing company concerned with the acquisition of raw materials, components or bought-out parts. It is a critical operation in the sense that the manufacturing programme depends on the availability of these components, so that ensuring availability/continuity of supply is often a key task for purchasing managers. This is usually achieved by dual-sourcing or multiple-sourcing, i.e., having more than one source of supply, sometimes tempting new manufacturers into the market to achieve this end, or locating additional sources of supply abroad. (See also *consignment stocking* and *just in time*.)

The purchasing operation is important in several other ways:

- the quality of the final product is in part dependent on the quality of the bought-out parts and materials (see *quality control*);

- the efficiency of the purchasing operation may have knock-on effects for the buying company in its delivery performance to its customers – put the other way, poor delivery performance is often caused by the late delivery of parts and materials disrupting the manufacturing programme (see *vendor analysis*);

- the cost of bought-out parts and materials is an important determinant of end cost – in fact considerable gains in price competitiveness or profit margins can sometimes be made by achieving quite modest reductions on supplier prices (see *discounts*).

The standing of the purchasing function has tended to rise in the cost-conscious 1980s, especially as the reduction of input costs has come to be seen as a more potent method of maintaining profitability than attempts to raise turnover or market share.

Q

Quality Circles   A Japanese institution now widely adopted in the West. Its essence is that small groups of production workers meet during company time to discuss quality issues and recent quality performance, perhaps under the non-directive leadership of a first-line supervisor or inspector. The presumption is that this raises quality consciousness, and that the mutual exchange helps to generate solutions to practical quality problems 'at the coal face'.

Quality Control   Its objective is the maintenance of quality standards, and the savings attendant on the reduction of scrap. This objective often involves three distinct operations:

(a)   goods inward control, or the inspection of raw materials or bought-out parts when they arrive at the factory;

(b)   medial inspection, or checking the quality standard of partly manufactured goods, often in the form of checking major manufactured components or sub-assemblies;

(c)   final inspection of finished products before their dispatch to the customer or launch into the distribution system.

In process industries (see *process production*) quality control is typically a laboratory based operation which takes the form of monitoring the process (rather than the product).
  ⁃ The alternative responses to these inspectional exigencies are:

(a)   inspect everything;

(b)   inspect nothing (and hope for the best);

(c)   practise statistic quality control (SQC): this is sample inspection where applied mathematics define the likelihood of defects in the proportion not inspected thereby offering calculable levels of protection.

The inclusion of (b) above, inspect nothing, is not frivolous: there is a survey evidence from Britain in the late 1970s suggesting that the number of firms practising the more sophisticated SQC is matched by the number doing nothing.
  A further ramification of quality control is that especially larger companies may inspect the quality control procedures of potential suppliers, perhaps even becoming involved in initial stages in the supplier's operations to raise standards. This is particularly likely where the size relativities make the buyer dominant (see quasi-*vertical integration*).
  Developments in quality control include:

• building quality into the system, i.e., using design, work organization, and production engineering skills to inhibit faults and defects;

• *quality circles* (see separate entry);

• placing responsibility for quality as much as possible with production workers themselves, even if (some) inspectors are employed as a 'second line of defence'.

But perhaps the most dramatic change has been the emergence of the conviction that the customer has a right to quality. Not so long ago there was a widespread view that just because you paid for it that did not mean you could expect it to work.

R

Ratio Analysis   A technique used in the interpretation of accounts, whereby figures in the accounts are related to each other in order to appreciate their significance. For example, if you were told Company X made an operating profit of £250,000 last year you would not, by contemplating this figure in isolation, be able to make any meaningful comment on the company's performance. If, however, you were also told that Company X employed total assets of £1,250,000 you would be able to compute a ratio of return on capital employed, being:

$$\frac{\text{Operating profit}}{\text{Total assets}} = \frac{250,000}{1,250,000} = 20\%$$

Thus you would now have a picture of what the company achieved compared with the total resources employed. This could be compared with:

- the company's own performance in previous years;

- the performance of other companies in the same industry;

- average ratios for a number of companies in the same industry;

- target ratios for the company.

A wide range of ratios can be computed to examine all aspects of a company's position.

Ratio analysis is a valuable tool, but must be used with some caution. This is because financial accounts do not necessarily give a full and fair representation of the economic reality of the position of a business.

See also *financial accounting*.

Red-Lining   Putting a (metaphoric) red line around certain areas where it is is believed that it is not in a company's interest to deal with them. Internationally it signifies barring some countries as potential recipients of exports or loans on account of their presumptive instability or lack of creditworthiness. Domestically it is a case of not providing goods or services on hire or credit for what are thought to be (usually urban) problem areas. A taxi driver who declines to take you into a rough area of town late on Saturday night is red-lining.

Redundancy   The situation where a job is lost because the employer no longer requires performance of that work. Redundancy has become increasingly common in the Western world because of both recession and technological developments.

Where redundancy arises in a business that continues to trade then in the UK management will often agree to offer incentives for 'voluntary' redundancy to workers who choose to terminate their employment early. Indeed, in some areas of the public sector in the UK it often happens that 'voluntary' redundancy terms are awarded when, in fact, the same job is to be recreated for a new employee in a slightly different guise.

Relations between Departments   Relations between the various functions and departments – sales, production, R & D, finance, and so on – often leave something to be desired. There is also an erroneous tendency to dismiss such interdepartmental tensions as personality clashes, and to prescribe 'better communications' as the cure-all. But it is important to grasp that the specialized competences of different departments give them different interests and 'war aims', independent of who staffs particular posts.

There are no guaranteed remedies, but interdepartmental strife may be reduced by:

- having thought-through policies which are known – having an explicit manufacturing policy, for instance, may eliminate many of the sales–production clashes;

- the traditional solution of co-ordination by hierarchy (i.e., when there is a disagreement someone higher up will decide) may be more effective if those higher up have a *more balanced* functional background (consider the over-representation in Britain of general managers with finance and marketing backgrounds);

- some of the nettles can be grasped in advance – if cash is a problem, for instance, then sooner or later a manufacturing manager won't be able to get components he needs because the supplier has not been paid for the last consignment;

- broadening the functional experience of middle management;

- role playing exercises.

Research and Development (R & D)   That function of a company concerned with scientific investigation aimed, at least in principle, at the generation of new products or improved processes and their translation into something usable. R & D departments tend to be a feature of larger and especially high-tech companies. The classic concerns surrounding the R & D function are:

- the recruitment of high quality researchers and their integration into a profit-making rather than academic milieu;

- the R & D – marketing interface, or a research initiative to produce what the market will buy;

- control of R & D projects in situations typically of high uncertainty: there are no rules which tell you when to spend another £100,000 or when you are on the edge of a breakthrough.

Research shows country-to-country differences in the amount spent on R & D, with Japan, for example, being high and slow to cut R & D spending in recessionary times. But there seems to be no simple relationship between R & D spending and commercial success, this depending rather on the marketing connection (see above) together with an efficient handling of the R & D-to-production transition.

Reservation of Title   When a business sells goods on credit terms the legal position, normally, is that those goods become the property of the customer at the time of sale. Thus if the customer fails to pay, and goes into liquidation, then the seller has no right to demand the goods back and ranks alongside other unsecured creditors. These unsecured creditors receive a share of any money the liquidator can raise from selling the assets of the bankrupt business after all the preferential and secured creditors have been paid in full.

The seller's position may be improved if the contract of sale incorporates a 'reservation of title' clause, whereby the seller reserves the right to recover the goods if payment is not made. Such clauses, often called *Romalpa clauses* after the legal case which set a precedent in this area (see separate entry), have to be drafted carefully to be legally valid. Moreover, some major companies simply refuse to purchase goods on these terms. However, the use of such a clause may be very attractive to the manager with a major bad debt problem.

Retail Operations   Successful chain or multiple retailing seems to centre on the pluses and minuses associated with centralization. There is clearly a case for centralization (and standardization), namely the advantages of central buying, centrally organized distribution, uniform pricing and standard store format, layout and range. And there is some evidence to suggest that centralization in retailing correlates with business success, though it does not in manufacturing. At the same time buyers must have flair and independence; they should be constrained only by the market and not by the management structure. In addition, the organization has to be imaginative enough to motivate salespeople: in retailing the selling is done by a lot of people at the bottom, not as in manufacturing by a few people at the top. The same problem is present at the store manager level: centralization will constrain these managers to conform, but the company also needs them to strive and compete.

Retirement Policy   Any enterprise needs to formulate a policy on the retirement of employees. This might include:

- *setting a retirement age* – for example, should this be fixed for all employees, thereby avoiding accusations of discrimination, or should it vary according to the required abilities for different jobs?

- *provisions for retirement benefits*, both in terms of pension scheme administration and any other employee benefits to which pensioners might be given access;

- *preparation of employees for retirement*, with possibly extended leave periods and pre-retirement courses.

Return on Capital Employed   This is an accounting ratio (see *ratio analysis*) which relates the profit earned by an enterprise to the resources employed. The ratio can be computed in a number of ways, but is most commonly measured as:

$$\frac{\text{Profit before tax} + \text{Interest payable (Return)}}{\text{Total assets (Capital)}}$$

This ratio can be investigated further by considering the 'secondary ratios' being:

(a)   Asset turnover, computed as:

$$\frac{\text{Sales}}{\text{Capital}}$$

This ratio tells us what level of activity the business generates from the assets employed.

(b)   Net profit percentage, being:

$$\frac{\text{Return}}{\text{Sales}}$$

This ratio tells us what profit is being earned from the activity of the business.

The use of secondary ratios can be a simple but powerful tool. To give a simple example, let us suppose that a company has suffered a drop in return on capital employed and one manager proposes to remedy this problem by tighter control over costs. If our secondary ratios showed no fall in the net profit percentage, with the poor results being entirely attributable to a fall in asset turnover, then we would be able to argue that the real problem did not lie in costs, which have not risen relative to sales, but in sales and production achieved.

Rights Issue   If a company wishes to issue new shares for cash, one way to do so is by means of a 'rights issue'. This involves offering existing shareholders the right to buy a certain number of new shares, in proportion to their existing shareholding, at a specified price. Normally the price will be set at a level below the current market price so that shareholders will have an incentive offer to buy the shares themselves or to sell this right to other people. Thus a rights issue will only be effective if either:

- existing shareholders are willing and able to buy at the specified price; or

- their shares are traded on the stock market, so that a market mechanism exists for shareholders to find other investors to buy their rights.

Ringi   A Japaness abbreviation understood in the West as signifying consensual decision-making. Its essence is:

- letting a lot of people have a (thoughtful) say;

- modifying original proposals to take account of critical comment (or showing the criticism to be invalid on the basis of additional staff work);

- putting up for top management approval and implementation a proposal which is as bombproof as human minds can contrive.

Ringi concedes to democracy without impairing hierarchy. It is the opposite of the stereotyped American 'What a great idea, let's do it!' It signifies slow decision-making (process of consensus) and fast implementation (teething troubles reduced, agreement secured in advance). But we should remember in the West that it is a culturally embedded form, and there are no rules on how to transpose it.

Risk   Many management decisions involve an assessment of future events where the outcome is uncertain, and where an adverse outcome may cause loss to the enterprise. The probability of loss is called 'risk'. An organization can reduce total risk by diversification, an idea that can be found in the Bible: 'Divide your merchandise among seven ventured, eight may be, since you do not know what disasters may occur on earth' (Ecclesiastes 11:2).

Experts in business finance use the term 'portfolio theory' to describe ideas on the diversification of risk.

Some risk involves ethical problems. For example, a manager may be faced with a decision as to whether to increase production at a small risk of straining plant capacity to the point where an accident may occur.

Younger managers keen to promote their careers by demonstrating good results tend to be more eager to take risks than older managers anxious to avoid putting their current job at risk.

Risky-Shift   A special case of *groupthink* (see separate entry) where groupthink denotes the tendency of groups to firm up on majority assumptions and exclude minority views. The essence of risky-shift is that decisions involving risk tend to be more adventurous (risky) when taken by groups than when taken by individuals. In the group setting, individuals get the impression that others are more daring than they are, decisional macho becomes the order of the day and individuals fail to voice their private fears.

The trouble is there is no rule that tells you when it is happening: spotting risky-shift 'on the ground' is a matter of experience and intuition.

Ritual There has been an increasing interest in ritual with the growing recognition of the importance of corporate culture. The connection is that ritual is seen as the expression of corporate culture, and as a means of reinforcing it (see *corporate culture* and *culture*). Ritual may also be used to reward and censure, as in the oft-quoted case of the retail chain where, at the annual convention, the ties of poor performing branch managers are cut off!

Role The concept refers to the expected and acceptable behaviours for incumbents of some particular status, for example, boss, secretary, salesman or research scientist. The concept is helpful in two ways. The first is analytic: it helps us to separate the job from some particular incumbent. It may well be the case that our production superintendent is famous as an amateur rose grower, and we can hardly imagine anyone doing his job who is not passionately fond of roses, but the concept of the *role* of production superintendent focuses our minds on the real constraints and dynamics of the job, independent of the personal vagaries of any particular occupant. The second way is diagnostic: we may be able to figure out what is going wrong in the execution of a management job by looking first at the role requirements, then at the individual performance, and noting disparities between them.

Role Conflict The orthodox meaning of the term is the situation where different people or groups hold contradictory expectations of the incumbent of a particular role. The classic case is the foreman where workers expect him to be 'one of them' while management regards him as part of management and subject to the same constraints and expectations as higher managers.

The secondary meaning of role conflict is when the same person occupies separate roles whose performance requirements or expectations are different/in conflict; this gives us the husband *v.* boss, 'lamb-in-the-home'/'lion-in-the-office' phenomenon. Probably the more serious if less entertaining manifestations of the role conflict in the secondary sense are where a diffuse professional identity is crossed with a specific work role, for instance, trained accountant and credit controller for X Ltd, educated sociologist and personnel officer for Y Ltd, and so on.

Role Playing A training technique where participants are obliged to 'play act' a role that they do not in real life occupy, usually interacting thereby with other trainees in related counter roles. Thus, for example, several trainees will act out, say, a wage negotiation situation, some acting for the company and others for the organized workers. Role playing is held to be particularly helpful for gaining an understanding of the other person's position by 'playing his hand', especially where that other person is one with whom, in role terms, one would have little sympathy. Hence it has value in sensitizing managers to the aims and expectations of blue-collar workers and their representatives, or in inducing some reciprocal understanding between representatives of functions, such as sales and production, which are often at loggerheads.

Romalpa Clause   A clause in conditions of sale which retains ownership over goods until payment is received, named after the *Romalpa* UK legal case which laid down the conditions under which such clauses could apply. See *reservation of title*.

S

Safety   The promotion of safe working practices is imposed by legal sanctions, and is also desirable to avoid production hold-ups and claims for damages and to promote good public relations. Safety measures cover both avoidance of specific accidents and protection from hazards that cause long-term damage to employees.

However, safety measures carry costs. In a UK case a manufacturer demonstrated to a trade union that the lower the level of asbestos usage in a process the higher the costs, and consequently the lower the level of employment. The union agreed to a higher level of asbestos usage than the ideal safety level.

Salesmen   These are the company employees directly concerned with *selling* (see separate entry).

Salesmen come from a wide variety of backgrounds, some highly qualified and some with no formal training. The good salesman needs to be:

- highly self-disciplined: by the nature of the job, the salesman spends most of the time working alone;

- able to get on with a wide range of people, for example, an industrial paint salesman will need to persuade the technical experts and the shop-floor workers, as well as the buying manager;

- capable of appreciating the technical characteristics of the product range;

- positive thinking, and resilient in the face of disappointments;

- perceived to be trustworthy: not only will the salesman need to be able to put forward representations about the product that are believed, he will also come to know a great deal of confidential information about the customer.

Sales Promotion   Sales promotion involves messages about the product to be circulated in media owned and controlled by the business itself (compare *advertising* – see separate entry). Such media include direct mail, exhibitions, point-of-sale displays and sales literature.

Sales promotion tends to be used 'tactically' to achieve short-term and limited objectives, e.g., to encourage consumers to sample a new product. This compares with advertising which tends to be used 'strategically' for such long-term objectives as creation of a brand image.

Saltsjöbaden   In 1938 in the Grand Hotel in Saltsjöbaden, a fiord-based resort outside Stockholm, momentous negotiations took place between the 'two sides of industry'. In the Swedish case these two sides were the confederation of (blue-collar) trade unions, invariably known by its initials LO, and its bargaining partner, the Swedish Employers' Federation, also widely known by its initials SAF.

Swedish industrial relations have not always been harmonious, and the 1920s in particular were a stormy period, but in practice the famous Basic Agreement at Saltsjöbaden changed all this.

The manifold details of this agreement covered such issues as grievance procedures, negotiating procedures, an early warning system for layoffs, the regulation of disputes, and so on. But more important than the procedural arrangements were the model and spirit of the agreement. The implicit model was that of the state (firmly Social Democratic by 1938) as non-interfering watch-dog so long as the contracting parties kept the peace. The spirit was one of mutual accommodation, bargaining and compromise.

Although there have been subsequent strains, this system has since served Sweden well. The expression Saltsjöbadensande (= the spirit of Saltsjöbaden) is a standard phrase in Swedish – like 'spirit of 1940' in English!

Sandwich Course   Term for any kind of educational course that involves periods of practical work experience 'sandwiched' between periods of full-time study. The 'thick' sandwich involves one complete year of work experience, the 'thin' sandwich several shorter periods.

Many degrees in management subjects involve such sandwich training. This gives employers an opportunity to see potential recruits in a practical work situation before committing themselves to permanent employment on graduation.

Scientific Management   A movement for the rationalization of manual work and increased output in the USA in the late nineteenth and early twentieth century. Its two principal exponents/practitioners were Frederick Taylor and Frank Bunker Gilbreth. There are several related elements:

- the development of time and motion study – timing jobs, timing their constituent parts, finding out how long a job *should* take, looking for ways of speeding it up;

- observing work systematically to devise ways to reduce the physical effort involved, recommend postural improvements or mechanical aids, better tools and better job preparation, again all with a view to raising output;

- the implementation of strong financial incentives for manual workers – strict piecework and dynamic variations on piecework where, for instance, the rate for completed units goes up when a certain number has been passed (e.g., £1 a piece for first 50, then £1.25 for next 20, then £1.50 above 70 on any given day) to maximize incentives at the upper end of the performance spectrum;

- the demonstration to employees that the piece rates are intended to allow very good workers to earn high wages over a sustained period of time, that high output and high economy will not lead to the rates being reduced.

Scientific management has survived in the form of the routine operation of time and motion study for rate fixing in many industries, ergonomics or the study of physical-mechanical aids to worker production, and in an ongoing interest in payment systems of a competitive and performance linked kind.

Scott Bader Commonwealth   An interesting example of a firm founded on idealistic principles of full worker participation and now owned by the workforce. Workers elect representatives onto the governing council of the company. Divisions between managers and workforce are seen as arising from functional differences rather than differences in social and economic interest.

The company has a code of practice which acknowledges a wide range of social responsibility, extending to:

'(1) Limiting the products of our labour to those beneficial to the community, in particular excluding any products, for the specific purpose of manufacturing weapons of war.

(2) Reducing any harmful effect of our work on the natural environment by rigorously avoiding the negligent discharge of pollutants.

(3) Questioning constantly whether any of our activities are unnecessarily wasteful of the earth's resources.'

Secondment   A manager may be offered an opportunity for secondment for a period of time to another part of the enterprise, possibly in another country. There can be real benefits both to the employer and the secondee in that the manager takes a new perspective to the place of secondment, and builds an awareness of the broader problems of the enterprise. However, the secondee should consider carefully whether on return to the home organization he is confident that he will not have suffered in terms of career prospects.

The manager may also have the opportunity for secondment to a customer or government department with which the business has dealings. Such experience may well increase the manager's value to his employer and so be a valuable career step.

In recent years a number of companies have developed the practice of seconding managers to help community organizations. Such a secondment is likely to provide substantial personal satisfaction to the manager concerned, but from a career point of view may need careful consideration.

Securities and Exchange Commission (SEC)   Body set up by legislation in the USA to oversee stock exchange behaviour. As an independent governmental body with considerable powers it offers an example that critics of the UK's self-regulation system often point to.

Securities and Investment Board (SIB)   A UK body set up by the Financial Services Act 1986. Members are appointed jointly by the Secretary of State for trade and the Governor of the Bank of England. The body is entrusted with the task of regulating the investment industry so as to protect investors. Being under the surveillance of the government, which can withdraw functions from it, the SIB does not possess the same independence as the *Securities and Exchange Commission* (see separate entry) in the USA.

Selection   The selection of new employees is one of the management roles that can least readily be approached with 'scientific' techniques because of the difficulty of objective evaluation. Broad stages in the selection process can be identified as follows:

- Analyse the job to be done, prepare a written description, and draft a job specification identifying the qualifications and personal qualities required. Each job vacancy offers the opportunity to reconsider the requirements for that job, which might well have changed since the previous employee was recruited.

- Recruitment involves a choice between internal advertising, selecting appropriate media for public advertising and possible use of an agency – or even 'headhunters'.

- Short listing on the basis of application forms involves assessing not only their information content but also the skill and confidence with which applicants present themselves.

- Interviewing is the most subjective part of the selection process and, in so far as the applicant will need to work well with members of the interview panel if appointed, this need be no bad thing. Good interviews include some 'open' questions, allowing time for applicants to pursue some issue in depth.

- References are used in various ways, sometimes being taken up prior to the interview as part of the assessment procedure and sometimes only being taken up after interview as a safety mechanism.

Selling Basically about getting the customer to buy the product. The selling process can involve a whole range of different tasks, depending on the situation. In its simplest form, the sales force may be little more than order takers, as in the case of a travelling salesman picking up orders from established retailers. At the other extreme, the salesman may be involved in a thorough analysis of an individual customer's particular needs. For example, a salesman selling high value capital equipment may need to understand the method of capital investment appraisal used by the customer, and be able to prepare detailed calculations to show that the product on offer will meet the customer's criteria.

Even where the salesman's role is basically restricted to taking orders, the salesman is important in presenting the image of the business. The salesman is also likely to be the first of the company's employees to hear of customers' attitudes to the product. We know of at least one successful company which insists that all new management recruits start off with one year working as salesmen, so as to have a clear view of how the company's customers think.

Servan-Schreiber, J.J. (1924–) Best known as the author of *Le Défi Américain* ('The American Challenge'). Servan-Schreiber identified a growing American domination of European business, both directly through investment and indirectly through the spread of American business methods. An essential of his proposed response is a move towards full integration, both economic and social, in the European Community. Of particular interest to European managers is another aspect of the analysis, that the great American strength has not been in availability of capital or technology but in managerial skills. These ideas have been widely quoted by advocates of European unity.

Shares Almost all companies are owned by shareholders; the rights of the various shareholders will be defined in the articles of association, the company's constitution. Sometimes a company has more than one class of share. Each share has two types of right attached:

(a) rights to share in the profits of the company;

(b) rights to vote on how the company should be managed.

The two main types of share are:

(a) *Preference shares.* These tend to enjoy a fixed rate of dividend, paid providing the company has available profits. Normally they only have voting rights on any proposal to change their status.

(b) *Ordinary shares.* These enjoy whatever rate of dividend the directors choose to 'declare' each year. In practice the rate of dividend often fluctuates in proportion to profits. Ordinary shareholders elect the directors, and vote on a variety of company business.

It is important to note that these brief descriptions are generalizations. To understand what rights a company's shares enjoy it is necessary to consult that

Shop Steward   A full-time employee, typically in manufacturing industry, charged by the relevant trade union with introducing new employees to the union and collecting union dues. This, however, is a rather formal definition, and in practice the shop steward represents the wants, wishes and above all grievances of the workforce to management. Supervisors, production managers and to a lesser extent personnel officers have most of their industrial relations related dealings with shop stewards rather than with outside union officials. There are a few things to keep in mind when dealing with shop stewards (as when negotiating with anyone):

- master the facts, especially the tedious circumstantial facts – the stewards will have done so;

- remember they don't always mean everything they say: shop stewards go in for trial balloons, cautious pressure and raising matters for a variety of tactical purposes – like everyone else;

- they will bring together unconnected things for bargaining purposes whenever it suits them;

- they will not be impressed by displays of formal cleverness (being clever means getting your own way, not spotting *non sequiturs* in the opponent's argument);

- they will 'redefine' issues when it suits them;

- they will exploit management weakness, both personal and structural.

Finally, there is no particular merit in bending over backwards to be reasonable. The goal is not to be in the right, but to win.

'Sitting by Nellie'   A training method whereby an employee is expected to learn by watching someone else doing a job – probably British industry's favourite training method! If the system is to work, 'Nellie' has to be both willing and able to explain to her pupil what she is doing and why.

It is important that management should be aware of situations where they are expecting training to occur in this way, so that the employee responsible for instruction is both motivated and equipped to do the job.

Skunk Works   Separate premises where R & D or new product development teams work on hopefully brilliant projects away from the constraints of the main company. When they have developed something good, they are brought back into the corporate mainstream to help with manufacturing methods and marketing plans.

Both the phrase and institution have been celebrated by Peters and Waterman in *In Search of Excellence* (see *excellence*). Praising the merit of the skunk works is part of the (re-discovered) emphasis on ingenuity and freedom rather than on structure and systems in management.

Social Responsibility   To what extent do the managers of a business have a responsibility to society as a whole, as opposed to their responsibility to the owners?

Milton Friedman has argued: 'Few trends could so thoroughly undermine the very foundations of our free society as the acceptance by corporate officials of a social responsibility other than to make as much money for their stockholders as possible.' Friedman's argument is based on the view that for business to adopt policies that diminish profit on grounds of 'social responsibility' results in less economic efficiency and therefore actually makes society poorer. .

A wide range of arguments are deployed against Friedman's view. One argument is that if managers follow socially undesirable policies then in the long run governments will legislate to control abuses. For example, it is argued that it is in the collective interests of the business community to act in a socially responsible way that minimizes legislative action. Other arguments question the efficiency of the market mechanism or suggest that economic efficiency is too narrow a goal.

Socio-Technical Systems Theory   An approach to understanding organizations developed by the Tavistock Institute of Human Relations in London during the 1950s and 1960s.

This approach views the organization as a system in the sense that:

- it is an entity with a boundary, distinct from its environment;
- it has an exchange relationship with the environment (imports manpower, raw materials, etc., and exports goods and services);
- it is made up of interdependent parts;
- these parts comprise especially a social or sentient system (groups doing work together) and a technical or task system (actions performed to accomplish output ends);
- these parts covary – a change in the technical system will be (naturally) accompanied by a change in the social system, and so on.

It has been a useful diagnostic tool for pinpointing cases of workforce malaise/task failure, particularly those relating to the implementation of technical change where the social consequences of such change for work-group structure had not been taken into account. This approach also focuses attention on the boundaries between the organization and its environment and between the parts of the system: exchanges across these boundaries may be critical.

Software Houses   These exist to sell systems design capacity/manpower to anyone who needs them. The market has undergone a significant change in the late 1980s in that industrial customers everywhere are going on to fixed-price projects (having noticed that time scales and budgets are generally over-run). At the same time, the industry is growing by around 30% p.a., which means both that it is easy to grow, and that any individual company achieving 30% is doing no more than holding on to its market share.

Also, the market is more differentiated than may be obvious to outsiders. Customers may want different things: the big prima donna customer may want flexibility, a willingness to respond to their instant need, whereas the average industrial customer will want 'heavy duty' software capacity plus the record for completion on time.

Customers also differ in their attitude to innovation. Defence agencies tend to be high tech, and want state-of-the-art solutions (and in the milieu of the late 1980s, so do banks) whereas industrial customers want tried and trusted solutions.

There is also some patterning of the market internationally. Opportunities are probably greatest in countries such as the Netherlands and Scandinavia, with their high social security costs per employee (and difficulty in firing people); such regimes favour consultancy services and buying in rather than employing your own.

Sourcing   See *purchasing*.

Span of control   A manager's span of control is the number of people who report directly to him. The concept figures large in the classical management literature where the emphasis is on restricting the span of control and thus keeping the manager's supervisory task within reasonable bounds. The principal theorist of limited span of control, V.A. Graicunas, carries the notion further by arguing that a manager is not only concerned with the relationship he has with each of his subordinates but must also take cognizance of the relationships between pairs of subordinates − this means that the supervisory complexity faced by a manager increases geometrically as additional subordinates are added to his span of control, a dynamic argument for holding the span of control to a maximum of five or six.

Subsequent thinking, however, suggests that the whole thing is much more relative. There is no absolute answer to the question of how many people a manager can supervise or have reporting to him. It depends on a range of factors: how mature and responsible they are, what work they perform, how far that work lends itself to control via exception reporting, what the organizational opportunities are for developing intersubordinate relations, and so on. It has also become clear that both manager and supervisor spans of control may vary on a national basis: research has shown that spans of control are typically wider in Britain than in France, and wider in West Germany than in Britain.

Sponsored Spin-Out Within a large company a promising business idea may have to be rejected because it does not fit within the company's overall business plan. A way round this problem is for a new company to be formed, with the parent company taking a financial stake and providing management back-up. Such a 'sponsored spin-out' allows the parent company both to share in the profits of the idea and to enjoy a continuing trading relationship with the new company.

Standards The performance level which is specified by management as the expected achievement for an aspect of the business. Thus a standard is a vital link between planning and *control* (see separate entry).

Star Term used by the *Boston Consulting Group* (see separate entry) to describe a product with a high market share and a high growth rate. Such a product is regarded as suitable for substantial investment to ensure that market share is maintained and expanded.

Status The phenomenon of status in formal organizations is often the subject of jocular (and rueful) comment both in everyday life and in a section of the literature, so that it is important to spell out its legitimate purpose. The most general argument is that in formal organizations, as in society at large, status differences are necessary for success and indeed survival. The high-status positions, that is, are marked by importance, difficulty or responsibility, such that relatively few people can fill them effectively. The possible rewards of status thus stimulate competition for such positions, and facilitate the emergence of able people.

In the company context we may also say that formal status is organizationally useful in that it indicates the nature of powers, responsibilities and functions. Similarly, status may be significant in that it authenticates communications for recipients and establishes priorities in execution. Status may aid the development of authority and responsibility; the enjoyment of high status, for example, may induce a sense of responsibility, a kind of organizational *noblesse oblige*, or dignify the exercise of authority.

With regard to individuals rather than the organization, status may also serve useful functions, for instance:

- achieving status may integrate an individual's personal history in the sense of being a justification of his expenditure of effort to achieve some advance;

- imputing high status to those who give orders may help to preserve the self-respect of those who take orders;

- the self-respect of relatively low status organizational members may be enhanced by imputing high status to top people who symbolize the organization, membership of which thus becomes a source of pride;

- status may even protect individuals from excessive claims – the high-status individual is protected from unnecessary disturbance, the low-status individual from excessive demands – at the same time status is a mechanism for the partial segregation of unequal individuals, enabling their co-operation but preventing mutual irritation.

Notwithstanding the foregoing analysis, status may sometimes be a barrier to communication, and it is noticeable that some managers choose to reduce the social distance between themselves and their subordinates to increase the flow of information upwards, and even more generally to 'get closer to' subordinates to be better able to influence them (see *hierarchy*).

Stewart, Rosemary   Distinguished member of the Oxford Management Centre, famous for a series of studies of the nature of management work. She has shown that:

- It is possible to show what managers do in a variety of tangible ways: how much time they spend alone, with their bosses and off-site, and with whom are their contacts, where do their deadlines come from, and so on.

- Management work is not monolithic; it makes a lot of difference what kind of manager (function, level and context) you are talking about.

- Even allowing for this, management jobs invariably present the individual with several choices: how much innovation; to control or develop subordinates; emphasize the technical or supervisory aspects of the job; and so on.

Stock Control   Any business that manufactures or deals in goods will need to hold stock. Management must ensure that the business has a satisfactory system to control and record stock holdings. Management must also decide maximum and minimum stock levels, bearing in mind such factors as:

- potential price fluctuations
- how much cash the company can afford to pay out on stock
- risks of deterioration
- risks of obsolescence, particularly in high-fashion industries
- storage and insurance costs
- what quantity of stock can most economically be ordered at one time (the economic order quantity)
- fluctuation of demand
- reliability of delivery by suppliers

Stock Exchange   A market where various kinds of security, mainly shares and loan stocks, are traded. By far the biggest in the world is the New York exchange. In size London comes third (after Tokyo). All major stock exchanges impose high compliance costs on listed companies in terms of such matters as disclosures to shareholders. Benefits to a company of such a listing include:

- the company has access to market mechanisms to raise finance from the general public;

- existing shareholders enjoy the benefit of being able to sell their shares easily;

- a market value for shares is established, easing negotiations with the Inland Revenue on share valuation;

- shares in a listed company can be used in offers for a takeover bid;

- employee share incentive schemes are easier to operate.

Stockist   An intermediary warehouse cum onselling institution. The stockist buys big lots cheaply from the manufacturer, and onsells them at a higher price, typically in small lots to small firms or other end-users.

Stockists help 'the world go round' by:

- simplifying the sales operation for manufacturers;

- offering a local source of supply to small buyers;

- acting as a buffer between the two, allowing manufacturers a more even throughput.

Strategic Analysis   The first stage in the formulation of *corporate strategy* (see separate entry). It involves consideration of how the *environment* (see separate entry) in which the organization operates has changed, assessment of the resources of the organization and an appreciation of the values and expectations of those involved in the organization. On the basis of this analysis a view can be formed as to how well placed the organization is to cope with the changes in its situation, and to what extent change is necessary.

See also *SWOT*.

Strategic Choice   In the management of *corporate strategy* (see separate entry) strategic choice involves:

- identification of a range of strategic options – at this stage management should be considering a broad range of options, based on strengths and weaknesses identified at the *strategic analysis* stage (see separate entry);

- evaluation of the range of strategic options, looking at their effects and at their feasibility;

- selection of a strategy – this is likely to involve delicate management judgements, without a clear-cut 'right' or 'wrong' answer.

119

Strategic Implementation   Once a business has decided on a *corporate strategy* (see separate entry) it is necessary to proceed to implementation. This is likely to involve planning the necessary allocation of resources, deciding on the responsibilities of existing departments, and reviewing the whole organizational structure. For example, if a long established business decides to invest heavily in a revolutionary new product some form of *intrapreneurship* (see separate entry) may be appropriate.

Stress Interview   A technique to find out what applicants are 'really like' and whether they have got what it takes, e.g., by hectoring, contradicting or insulting them. It is probably self-defeating as well as socially undesirable.

There are, however, some jobs such as air traffic control, where ability to stand stress is so critical it has to be tested in the selection process, but this is usually achieved in a formal, laboratory-test way rather than by such forms of interpersonal violence.

Or again, there are some jobs focusing on the degree of specialist knowledge where one can only find out how much a person knows by pursuing a line of questioning to the point where they cannot answer (like designing examinations where no-one can get 100% so that it is always possible to compare the performance of individual candidates).

Subcontracting   Passing on some of the work of a manufacturing company to outside contractors, usually smaller companies. Strictly speaking, there are two forms: first, subcontracting by process where the company has outsiders performing particular operations, for instance, chromium plating of metal components. Second, the company may pay other firms to do things that it can and is doing itself. The purpose here is usually to preserve the balance between workforce capacity and available work: when peaks occur you give more work to the subcontractors, when there are troughs, you take it away from them, but your own workforce always has enough to do. Subcontracting sometimes becomes an industrial relations issue where shop stewards claim a company should offer regular overtime to its own employees before engaging in the second type of subcontracting.

Supplier Power   Term used to describe the factors which give the supplier strength in negotiating with a buyer. See also *buying power*.

Sweden   By the conventional measure of GNP per capita, Sweden is one of the richest countries in the world, coming before the USA, Japan and West Germany. Like Germany there is a strong engineering tradition with emphasis on product development, manufacturing methods and quality (see *Technik*). As with Switzerland and Holland, there is a strong export orientation, and English speaking ability is widespread. Distinctive features include:

- long-term co-existence of parliamentary socialism and capitalist industry;

- strong co-determination system, based on worker representatives' right to negotiate on any issues of their choosing;

- low unemployment rate, lots of retraining initiatives and sheltered workshops for the disabled;

- low wage differentials, low income spread, high personal taxation – managers are poorly paid by international standards with low fringe benefits and relative absence of material incentives;

- low interfirm mobility and low geographic mobility;

- egalitarian manners, and a cult of quiet competence.

An overriding feature of Sweden is low social differentiation, so that there is a much higher level of sex equality than in Britain or the USA; class is also a weak behavioural construct providing little help in marketing campaigns. See also *Saltsjöbaden*.

Switching Costs   The costs an enterprise faces if it switches from one supplier of goods and services to another. For example, a grocer who moves from one wholesaler to another faces a negligible switching cost. By contrast, a motor dealer who switches from one car manufacturer to another faces major costs in retraining staff, restocking with spare parts and new tools and with advertising. The higher the switching cost, the stronger the power of the supplier. See also *buying power*.

SWOT   A simple acronym standing for 'strengths, weaknesses, opportunities and threats'. A SWOT analysis combines an appraisal of the company's own strengths and weaknesses with an assessment of the opportunities and threats posed by the environment. SWOT offers a framework for *strategic analysis* (see separate entry).

Synergy   A synergistic effect takes place when by a combination of resources the total output achieved is greater than the sum of what could be achieved by the use of those resources individually. A manager must recognize this potential when deploying staff, in that there may be opportunities to improve output by creating work-groups of staff with complementary strengths.

T

Takeover Panel   A voluntary organization drawing its members from bodies concerned with investment and finance, the Takeover Panel administers the City Code on takeovers and mergers. The Panel has no legal powers, but transgressors who fail to comply are liable to encounter difficulties with the Stock Exchange which may suspend a share quotation or refuse listing for new securities.

Task Force   A group of managers and staff specialists, often drawn from a variety of organizational levels and functions, who collectively apply themselves to a particular assignment for the duration. The assignment is typically something both important and not quite routine – major organizational change, moving to a new site, bringing major facilities on stream or a takeover, merger or integration.

Advantages include:

• pooling disparate talents and experience

• underlining the importance of the mission by freeing task force members from their normal duties

• getting impetus from the *esprit de corps* of the task force.

The disadvantages are:

• the task force sometimes gets institutionalized and 'runs out of steam';

• not all companies can cope with the cross-rank, cross-function composition of the task force – there is a premium on flexibility as well as energy.

Tavistock Institute   The Tavistock Institute of Human Relations in north London is a research and consultancy organization. It is known in particular for the development of *socio-technical systems theory* (see separate entry) and its application to practical problems in industry, especially those resulting from the introduction of technical change.

Taxation   Managers are concerned with taxation in three different ways:

(a)   A business is often required to act as an unpaid collector of tax. Examples include deduction of PAYE on employees' remuneration and collection of VAT charged to customers. If the business does not have an adequate system to cope with this collection, and to respond promptly to changes in tax law, then any failure to collect tax as required may result in the business becoming liable for the shortfall.

(b)   The business may be liable for taxation on its own activities (see *corporation tax*).

(c)   Changes in tax law may have a substantial influence on the operations of the market in which the business operates. For example, car manufacturers keep a careful watch on changes in the ways in which company car users are taxed.

Taylor, Frederick W.   Founder of the scientific management movement. Born into a middle-class Pennsylvania family, he was prevented from going to college by poor eyesight and instead did an apprenticeship in the mechanical engineering industry. This led to an interest in the rationalization of manual work and the development of time and motion study together with incentive payment systems. Taylor is also associated with the idea of functional foremanship, which involves separating out the technical and work preparation aspects of foremanship from the supervisory, and vesting them in different people. Though the idea of functional foremanship in the pure Taylor sense was not widely taken up, it has presaged changes in the organization of production in the form of separate work study units, production control/scheduling departments, tool rooms, and the separate administration of piecework earnings. See *scientific management*.

Technik German word that denotes the knowledge and skill relevant to manufacture, that is, the mix of engineering knowledge and craft skill.

The idea of *Technik* serves as a rallying point for all those connected with manufacture, and sustains the status of the production function and related technical departments.

There is no real equivalent in English, 'technology' lacking the folksy ring of *Technik*, and 'technique' being too general a word. The idea, however, is not exclusively Germany, with *Teknik* in Swedish and *Techniek* in Dutch, for example, expressing the same idea.

In the late 1980s the word became very familiar in Britain through the Audi car advertisements slogan *Vorsprung durch Technik*, which may be translated as 'competitive advantage through superior engineering'.

Telephone Studies of how managers actually spend their time in both Germany and the UK have shown that some 10% of time is spent on the telephone. Thus for the successful manager it is important to cultivate a good telephone technique, both in terms of manner on the telephone and recording key points afterwards.

Theory X and Theory Y The 1950s and 1960s are an interesting time with regard to theories of motivation. The period was one of growth, prosperity and full employment, with the manufacturing sector still dominant over the tertiary sector and with a prevalence of semi-skilled workers. In this situation the efficacy of purely financial incentives declined and there was a blossoming of studies and theories pointing up the importance of non-monetary incentives, known collectively as the *neo-human relations* movement (see separate entry).

A central figure in this movement is the American academic, Douglas McGregor, whose book *The Human Side of Enterprise* (McGraw Hill, New York, 1960) counterposed Theory X and Theory Y. Theory X is all that can be inferred from the scientific and classical management schools about the drives and behaviour of the employee: he is lazy, needs close supervision, and has no interest in his work; his output can be raised only by ergonomic improvements in the job process accompanied by mounting financial incentives.

This old-style received wisdom is contrasted by McGregor with Theory Y in which people are viewed more positively:

- they are not basically lazy, they do want to work and will do so if they are treated right;

- people are able to develop, to take responsibility, to use initiative and to make decisions;

- people can be self-motivated and self-controlled and will work towards organizational goals if management create suitable conditions and opportunities.

The neo-human relations movement in general emphasized social and status needs of employees, self-fulfilment and intrinsic satisfaction. See also *Herzberg* and *Maslow's need hierarchy*.

Theory Z The expression coined by William Ouchi of the University of California's Graduate School of Management in his leading book of the same name (*Theory Z*, Addison-Wesley, Reading, Mass., 1981). It is part of the American response to the Japanese successes of the 1980s.

Ouchi's view is that the focus of Western interest should be on Japanese management style and corporate culture, contrasting as they do with what is prevalent in the USA. Indeed Ouchi believes that if American companies are going to respond to the Japanese challenge they will have to combine the best of the two management traditions, taking from the Japanese their emphasis on the collective, group loyalty, co-operation and generalism.

Part of the interest of Ouchi's ideas is that they are typical of the American response to Japanese economic hegemony in two ways. First, the USA, as the dominant economic power in the post World War Two period, takes the Japanese challenge more seriously than, for instance, Britain, for whom Japan is just the most recent in a succession of countries whose economic achievements are to be admired. Second, it is interesting that American commentators generally put the emphasis on these cultural and stylistic aspects of Japanese management: this is not universally the case – the Dutch, for instance, put the emphasis on particular Japanese practices such as quality circles and JIT.

Third World See *developing countries*.

Time Span of Discretion The time between an employee doing something and having it checked by higher authority, or between a person making a decision and having it or its consequences reviewed by superiors. It is the invention of British industrial psychologist Elliott Jacques, who saw it as a criterion for classifying jobs and awarding differential payments.

It is an important indicator of the demands and responsibility level of jobs, and a useful discriminator. It cannot, however, be used alone to characterize jobs, and it is vitiated in practice by the fact that, although the time span is held to be a property of the job, this is importantly affected at management level by the personality and strengths of particular job incumbents.

Top Management Executive members of boards of directors or the layer of general management at the top of operating companies. At this level there is a need for strategic sense and for at least a leaven of cool, rational planners, as opposed to the energetic, intuitive wheeler-dealers who often predominate in middle management.

Trades Council In the UK most towns and districts have a 'trades council' representing local trade union branches. Trades councils act as local co-ordinators of trade union activity. They do not tend to be involved in direct negotiations, but are often accepted by both central and local government as sources of nominations of trade union representatives to public bodies.

Most trades councils register with the *Trades Union Congress* (see separate entry), which exerts substantial influence on them. However, trades councils should not be regarded as TUC 'branches'.

Trades Union Congress (TUC) The TUC is a British association of trade unions, each of which retains its own independence. The TUC exercises influence rather than power over affiliated unions. Major functions of the TUC are to provide research and publicity services for the union movement as a whole, to formulate and articulate policies for the promotion of trade union interests, and to investigate and resolve disputes between member unions.

See also *Bridlington Agreement*.

Training An aspect of the personnel function concerned with helping workers acquire the skills needed for their job, prepare them for career development, and help them fit into the organization's structure. Training is sometimes regarded as a narrowly vocational activity, in contrast with the broader aims of education. However, a full training programme for an enterprise will include the cultivation of qualities of leadership and initiative in managers.

Training Commission Proposed new name for UK *Manpower Services Commission* (see separate entry).

Transfer Pricing The price at which goods or semi-manufactured goods are transferred between different parts of the same company. It arises typically where the produce of one part of a company is consumed as components or input to the manufacturing operation of another part. It is at its most complicated in the case of multinationals where the exchanges are cross country and cross currency.

Because the transfers are internal they do not have to be at market price; the transfer is an internal accounting exercise which may be made to serve a variety of goals. Indeed there are several considerations which may lead companies not to transfer at market price:

- manipulating transfer price enables manipulation of profitability – this may have a political/cosmetic value by, say, reducing revealed differences in profitability between different product lines or operating divisions;

- it may be employed as a weapon against blue-collar wage demands, serving to artificially reduce profitability in some part of the company thereby undermining wage demands;

- it can be used too in multinationals to concentrate profits in countries where the profits are most easily sheltered or corporation tax is low.

Apart from possible ethical objections another price may be paid for the manipulative use of transfer pricing. This is that profitability is used by management to evaluate the performance of operations, divisions and senior managers in charge of them. But if these profitability figures are debased through transfer pricing manipulation, then management is simultaneously debasing a diagnostic tool and evaluative method; it may also dilute the motivation of senior managers to prove themselves in terms of the profit performance of their business unit.

Trist, Eric   Leading figure in the Tavistock Institute of Human Relations in London. See *Tavistock Institute*.

U

Unit Production   Making items in ones, as opposed to in batches or in long runs. Bespoke tailoring is an ideal type of unit production operation.

Unit production usually puts a premium on a company's design capability and on work organization flexibility. It implies a skilled workforce, together with supervisors who can show and help rather than control and order.

Unit Trust   Offers investors the opportunity to buy 'units' representing holdings in a portfolio of securities handled by a management company. The investor buys in at a price that includes an initial charge for management costs, generally up to 5%, and each year management expenses are charged against the trust income. Unit trusts can be designed to specialize in certain areas, e.g., by geographic region, industrial sector, income yield or capital growth. The investor gains the benefit of expert professional management and a well spread investment.

While management companies frequently claim to have a record of 'beating the market', academic studies have tended to find that over the years most unit trusts do not tend to perform better than the market as a whole.

Unlisted securities market (USM)   Set up in the UK in November 1980, the USM is a separate and distinct market within the Stock Exchange. The costs of access to the USM are much lower than those involved in obtaining a full listing on the Stock Exchange, and the requirements to be complied with are less onerous. Thus the USM gives the smaller, growing company easier access to the capital markets. Once a company is admitted to the USM, it is also easier to progress to a full Stock Exchange listing.

USA   The world's largest economy and biggest market, the inventor of business schools and MBAs, and the source of most of the good quotes about business. Ironically, though most of the world's books about management have been written by Americans, they have not sought to offer an explicit picture of management in their own country, so we depend on the observations of foreigners with experience in the USA for a characterization. Things which strike business visitors include:

- a strong marketing orientation

- an attachment to the philosophy and apparatus of professional management

- strong on target setting, monitoring and financial control

- results oriented, but inclined to a short-term perspective

- anti-trade union, and hostile to European notions of co-determination

- takes the Japanese very seriously (see *Japan*).

Style and dress are generally informal by European standards. Opinions differ on whether American management is genuinely (and effectively) more hardworking, or just puts in long hours and keeps up a charade of hyperactivity.

V

Value   In making decisions managers will frequently need to have an estimate of the value of a resource to be consumed. It is important to be aware that any professional valuation of an asset depends on the instructions on condition and use given to the valuer. As an example, we recently spoke to a bank manager who had been shown by a client two different valuations on a property, one at £200,000 and one at £600,000. On investigation it turned out that a large part of the difference rested on different assumptions about permitted use of the property.

Value for Money   Phrase used to cover the relationship between economy, efficiency and effectiveness. It is commonly used in relation to public sector management, particularly in local government. Since 1982 local government auditors have been specifically required to investigate 'value for money' achieved.

Economy refers to the inputs used in an activity. Thus the more cheaply an activity is conducted, the greater the economy achieved.

Effectiveness is concerned with outputs. The more successfully an activity is conducted, the higher the degree of effectiveness achieved.

We can see that neither economy or effectiveness is in itself much of an indicator of achievement in public sector management, since economy is easy to achieve if quality of output is ignored and effectiveness is easy to achieve if costs of inputs are ignored.

Efficiency links these two ideas, being measured in principle by the ratio:

$$\frac{\text{Output}}{\text{Input}}$$

The problem here is that outputs are difficult to measure, particularly when we are considering organizations whose objectives are other than commercial. For example, we might measure the efficiency of a department of a hospital by comparing the number of operations performed (output) with the costs of the department (input). However, our measure of output is a substitute for patient satisfaction, which might actually be increased if fewer operations were performed as a result of alternative treatment being successful.

Public sector managers might often find 'value for money' used as a catch phrase to cut their budgets. It is useful to be able to argue that in some circumstances extra inputs might generate greater outputs, so that improved 'value for the money' may involve *increased* spending.

Vendor Analysis   The term given to a company's evaluation of other companies who sell to it. Most companies claim to do vendor analysis, but on closer inspection this offer turns out to be 'all in the mind' rather than a formal system. But given a sufficient scale of operations it is worth doing vendor analysis systematically, especially as it involves keeping track of the quality performance and punctuality of suppliers.

Venture Capital   An ill-defined term: broadly speaking it is used to describe money invested in new high-risk businesses. Venture capital funds invest in a range of such businesses, hoping by *diversification* to reduce *risk* (see separate entries).

Vertical Integration   Phrase referring to the strategy of some companies in moving backwards or forwards along the chain of interlocked operations, usually by acquisition. Most common is vertical integration backwards, where a manufacturing company buys suppliers of raw materials, components or sub-assemblies, but it may also take a forward form where the manufacturing company buys wholesalers, stockists or retail outlets, or even transport companies, PR or advertising agencies. The gain is in control and reliability, especially on the supply side. The corresponding disadvantage is that the company which is the initiator of the integration is taking on board the problem of matching a lot of inputs and outputs along the chain of operations. A manufacturer that pays a trucking company to deliver its goods, for instance, does not need to worry about whether it is using the entire capacity of the trucking company; but if that same manufacturing concern buys the trucking company it must match capacities, or solve the mismatch by 'slimming' the trucking firm or letting it deploy 'excess capacity' on the open market. Adjustments of this kind may well take the manufacturer into the control of operations in which it lacks expertise.

A British marketing academic, Keith Blois, has pointed to a variation on this theme of integration by acquisition, which he designates as *quasi-vertical integration*. This is when the initiating company achieves a substantial control over suppliers or distributors, primarily because of the purchasing power relativities in its favour, without actually acquiring them. A garment retail chain which takes 95% of the output of a company making shirts, for example, is able to dominate the shirt supplier, demanding favours in the form of priority delivery, credit terms and even stock holding costs.

Thus the advantage of quasi-vertical integration, for the dominant partner, is the advantages that control confers without the liabilities of ownership, in that the dominant company can 'love them and leave them' when such a procedure suits its needs. There is an arguable cost to society in that quasi-vertical integration represents an invisible increase in the power of corporate giants together with a real decline in competition.

VIE (valence, instrumentality, expectancy) Theory   See *expectancy theory*.

Voting Rights   In a company more than one class of share may be issued. Each class of share may have different rights to dividends and different voting rights. The most common type of shareholding structure is that all shares have the same rights, both in terms of dividends and voting. However, during the 1980s there has been a growing tendency in the USA for corporate managements to retain ownership of voting shares themselves while issuing non-voting shares to the general public, partly as a protection against takeover bids. In the UK during the 1980s a number of ingenious company voting structures have been designed when financing new small businesses. Thus when dealing with a company it may be important to identify, from the articles of association, where voting power lies.

W

Wage Councils   In the UK successive governments have set up wage councils for a number of individual industries. Generally these have been created for industries where there are a large number of employees making normal wage bargaining difficult. A wage council normally includes representatives of three groups: the employers, the unions and independent members appointed by the government. Currently the wage council system is under attack by critics who see it as leading to wage awards above market levels, with the consequence that workers are 'priced out' of jobs. Defenders of the system see it as protecting workers in industries, where union bargaining power is weak, from exploitation.

West Germany West Germany has been of interest from an economic and management viewpoint, though with an apparent contradiction.

West Germany is very successful economically: following the defeat and devastation of World War Two, vigorous reconstruction led to the emergence of an economically sound state, so that Germany is now the largest economy in Europe and one of the richest countries in the world. Germany has also tended to do better than her European neighbours: in the 1960s when everyone had prosperity the Germans had an 'economic miracle'; in 1974 when most of Europe was reeling under the effects of the first oil crisis, West Germany had its biggest trade surplus to date; in the recession of the early 1980s, unemployment figures rose later in Germany, did not rise so high, and started to go down more quickly than in neighbouring countries, and so on.

At the same time German management does not seem to outsiders to be especially sophisticated or professional: the German company is run by a committee (*Vorstand*); German companies tend to be weak on goals, mission statements and 'what business are we in' soul-searching; the professional management approaches and staff support are less developed than in the USA; there are no business schools, no MBAs nor really any undergraduate courses in management (degrees in business economics are the nearest approach).

So, how do they do it? Probably the most important answer is the apparently natural German enthusiasm for making things and for everything technical. Most German managers are engineers, engineering education is excellent, the technical functions including production tend to have higher standing than in Anglo-Saxon countries, and design is often the prima donna function. German companies typically expect to sell on the basis of the product quality plus delivery plus after-sales service. *Vorsprung durch Technik* is as much a national claim as an Audi slogan (see *Technik*).

To this technical and production orientation should be added a generally well-trained and strike-free workforce. Apprenticeship training is widespread and well regarded (there is a recognized apprenticeship for nearly 500 jobs); in some industries a semi-apprenticeship for semi-skilled jobs exists. Most foremen, in addition, are technically qualified. A combination of strong trade unions, orderly wage bargaining, economic growth plus legally binding pay settlements, together with Western Europe's oldest worker democracy system, have for the most part rendered the German workforce technically co-operative and stoppage free.

Finally, there is a meritocratic, achievement-oriented strain in German society, and this national emphasis on *Leistung* ('performance', 'achievement') has constructively suffused industry and management (Peter Lawrence, *Managers and Management in West Germany*, Croom Helm, London, 1980).

White Knight   Sometimes a company is faced with a takeover bid that is difficult to resist. An alternative to simply fighting to stay independent is to look for a 'white knight', an alternative bidder whose aims are regarded as more compatible with those of the existing management.

Wildcat Strike   A sudden or unexpected strike. Although both media and management often purport to be taken by surprise by strikes, many of them are loosely predictable in the sense of occurring at particular times of year (air traffic controllers strike in the summer, power workers in the winter) or in recognizable circumstances (annual pay bargaining). But in contrast, a wildcat strike is one that takes everyone by surprise.

Winning Streak, The   Title of book by Walter Goldsmith and David Clutter-buck (Weidenfeld and Nicolson, London, 1984) on the characteristics of top performing British companies and their leaders. A self-styled British sequel to Peters and Waterman's *In Search of Excellence*; not as good as the American trail-blazer, but well worth reading.
   See *excellence*.

Woodward, Joan   English sociologist, famous for a study of corporate structure in the 1950s. With a sample of over 100 companies from south-east Essex she was able to show that:

- there are lots of variations in company structure;

- they are not accounted for simply by size;

- that the three basic production types – unit production, mass production, process production – have distinctive structural forms;

- that within these three groups the more commercially successful companies appear to be those which are closest to the structural norms for their production type.

   Woodward's findings were dramatic at the time. Previously people had assumed that manufacturing companies would have broadly similar organizational structures, any structural differences simply reflecting size gradations. Her work also had a practical thrust, indicating appropriate structures for industries based on different production methods. The research is written up in her book *Industrial Organization: Theory and Practice* (Oxford University Press, 1965).

Work   The key insight that has emerged about work is that people do it for more than just the money, at least in most cases (see *human relations*, *Maslow's*

131

need hierarchy and *neo-human relations*). In a famous American study people were asked if they would continue to work even if they did not have to financially – the majority said they would. Their reasons included:

- the need to keep occupied
- they would feel lost without it
- they enjoy work
- it keeps you healthy

and so on: the common man's version of neo-human relations theory!

Worker Director   A worker/trade union representative sitting on the board/ executive committee. This may arise in countries with a strong co-determin- ation system such as West Germany, or in some socialist countries, for instance Yugoslavia. Worker directors were mooted as a possibility in Britain in the Bullock report in the late 1970s, but the Bullock recommendations were never implemented.

Working Capital   A term used in a variety of ways, including:

- the assets and liabilities of the business that are constantly exchanged during the course of trade, examples are debtors, creditors and stock;
- all the current assets and current liabilities of the business;
- the cash resources of the business.

Thus any manager who hears the term 'working capital' used should ascertain exactly what is meant by the speaker.
    See also *capital*.

Works Committee   Although there is no nationwide system of co-determin- ation in Britain, and no legal requirement for companies to have a *works council* (see separate entry), many companies of their own volition have established some such employee representative or consultative body, for which works committee is the most common name. The essence of such a works committee is that it meets in a regular, scheduled way and not in response to a crisis. It is typically chaired by a production or general manager, and discusses issues of common interest. Unofficially such committees tend to be used as downward communication channels by management, more than as genuinely consultative bodies.

Works Council   A worker representative committee of the type required by law in various European countries, for example, the *Betriebsrat* in West Germany or the *ondernemingsraad* in the Netherlands.

Works Director   A production manager, typically one in charge of a whole works or manufacturing site, with non–production functions such as sales and R & D located elsewhere.

Work Study   Involves the examination of all the aspects of a human work task. The objective is to investigate all the factors that influence the way a job is performed in order to identify opportunities for improvement.

Two techniques are used in work study: 'method study' and 'work measurement'. Method study involves a detailed analysis of the existing method of working, with a view to developing a more efficient method. Work measurement involves establishing the time for a qualified worker to carry out a specified job at a defined level of performance.

Z

Zero-Based Budgeting   In principle the presumption that no money is required under any budget heading until a case for expenditure has been developed. It is a cost-cutting, think-through-the-real-needs antidote to the convention of taking last year's budget and adding on a bit for inflation and a bit for good measure to construct the coming year's budget.